Hope in Christ
Finding Joy in the Midst of Despair

Greg Grotewold

Foreword by Dr. Henry Brandt

Copyright © 2005 by Greg Grotewold

Hope in Christ
by Greg Grotewold

Printed in the United States of America

ISBN 1-597811-73-4

All rights reserved solely by the author. The author guarantees all contents are original and do not infringe upon the legal rights of any other person or work. No part of this book may be reproduced in any form without the permission of the author. The views expressed in this book are not necessarily those of the publisher.

Unless otherwise indicated, Scripture quotations are taken from the *New American Standard Bible*®. Copyright © 1960, 1962, 1963, 1968, 1971, 1972, 1973 by The Lockman Foundation. Used by permission.

Scripture references marked (LB) are taken from the *Living Bible*®. Copyright © 1971 by Tyndale House Publishers. Used by permission.

www.xulonpress.com

Contents

Credits vii
Foreword ix
Prologue xiii

Part I—God's Glory, Our Delight

1. Hanging on by a Thread—Self-sustained Joylessness 19
2. Jesus—Our Deliverer 29

Part II—Meeting Us at the Point of Our Obedience

3. Taking Out the Garbage 35
4. Securing True Love 45
5. Forfeit to Win 53
6. Running on Empty 63
7. Obediently Joyful 73
8. Delighting in Him 81
9. To the Ends of the Earth and Back 91
10. The Big Miracle in the Little Man 103
11. Finding the Real Jesus 119
12. Filling the Void 127

13.	To Die is Gain—Coming Full Circle	139
14.	The Simplicity of the Gospel	143
15.	A Final Word	149

Contacting Us 155
Notes 157

Credits

The inspiration for *Hope in Christ: Finding Joy in the Midst of Despair* is Jesus Christ, the Author and Perfecter of our faith (Hebrews 12:2). He is the hero in this book. For without Him we would have no hope and therefore no reason to pen these words.

This project would never have come to life were it not for the love and support of my faithful wife, Sandi. I have been the beneficiary of much joy because of her steadfast obedience to God.

The construction of this book has not been an individual endeavor. It required the efforts of many to bring it to a successful conclusion. I want to thank, in particular, Sarah Cassada. Her commitment to making this publication a reality is deeply appreciated.

Foreword

Several years ago, I conducted a lecture series on marriage to about one hundred college students. To satisfy my own curiosity, I asked the class if any of their families had been hit by divorce. Every one of them raised their hands.

By contrast, in 1936, out of my high school graduating class of nearly one hundred students, virtually no one had ever heard of the word "divorce," much less been impacted by it. What a change in so short a time.

But there is hope. You have in your hands a wonderful book written by Greg Grotewold about Rebuilder Ministries. It details the dramatic change that occurs when you look at life from God's viewpoint rather than from your own.

As Greg points out, more and more often in our day, people try to eliminate misery and stimulate joy by means of drug use, "whether the 'drug' is sex, food, alcohol, cocaine, sleep, or relationships." "Whatever the hypnotic," he explains, "when used illicitly or excessively—that is, outside of God's intent—it is employed to inhibit reality." This seemingly easy solution in fact only leads to greater misery.

Fortunately, there is another source of help, upon which this book is based. The Apostle James writes in James

3:17-18 (LB): "But the wisdom that comes from heaven is first of all pure and full of quiet gentleness. Then it is peace-loving and courteous. It allows discussion and is willing to yield to others; it is full of mercy and good deeds. It is wholehearted and straightforward and sincere. And those who are peacemakers will plant seeds of peace and reap a harvest of goodness." It is refreshing just to think about such an environment. The good Lord beckons—no, pleads—to a wayward soul: "Oh, that you had listened to my laws! Then you would have had peace flowing like a gentle river, and great waves of righteousness . . . Yet even now, be free from your captivity!" (Isaiah 48:18, 20, LB).

There it is! The choice is yours! You can turn to the world to find relief, or you can turn to the Creator of the world for your peace!

Dr. Henry Brandt

**In memory of my dear sister, Jill,
whose hope was never found.**

Prologue

This book is built on 2 Corinthians 5:18-19: "Now all these things are from God, who reconciled us to Himself through Christ, and gave us the ministry of reconciliation, namely, that God was in Christ reconciling the world to Himself, not counting their trespasses against them, and He has committed to us the word of reconciliation."

It was written generally for anyone who is not perfectly satisfied in the Lord our God; namely, everyone. We all fall short of fully trusting and savoring our Savior; and therefore, we also fall short of experiencing His tremendous blessings. However, I had one particular group of people in mind as I crafted the language: the hopeless—individuals who have been unable to find any semblance of sustainable joy and whose moments of peace are far too infrequent and evaporate far too quickly.

The book traces the path of Chuck Raichert and the Rebuilder Ministries. Its mission is to reconcile relationships and restore lives by having people see their circumstances from God's perspective rather than their own limited frame of reference. As you will quickly gather, there is hope, regardless of the situation in which you currently find yourself. My prayer is that this book will be an encouragement and that your walk with Christ will be strengthened. Or, if you don't know Christ as Savior, that you will feel led to invite Him into your life.

While the stories in this book are true, the names of those that Chuck has ministered to, along with their respective family members and most acquaintances, have been changed in order to protect confidentiality.

And to try to be happy by being admired by men, or loved by women, or warm with liquor, or full of lust, or getting possessions and treasures: that turns you away, soon, from the love of God; then men, women, and drink and lust and greed take precedence over God; and they darken His light.... And then we are unhappy and afraid and angry and fierce, and impatient, and cannot pray, and cannot sit still. That is the bitter yoke of sin: and for this we leave the mild and easy yoke of Christ.[1]

Thomas Merton

Part I

God's Glory, Our Delight

God desires you to be joyful and experience sustainable delight (Psalm 16:11, 30:11-12, 37:4; Philippians 4:4; Job 22:25-26).

This is important to the Lord because He loves you and wants only the best for His creation. There's another reason, though, that is even more significant. When we become completely and wonderfully satisfied in Him alone for our every need, we not only gain peace but also fulfill our purpose for being created—to glorify our Creator. God made you so that you might exalt Him. We do this by delighting in Him and basking in His unparalleled splendor.[2] It's a masterful plan. He receives the adoration and we the blessing.

1

Hanging on by a Thread— Self-sustained Joylessness

Being joyful is not a mere fringe benefit; it is the very core of your existence in Christ. Why is it that so many Christians aren't? Many are not only without joy; they are in perpetual despair.

The range and depth of the despondency is as varied as the individuals who shoulder it. For some, the depression comes and goes; for others, it's a constant companion. The thread that ties them together is not merely the presence of pain, for we all experience periods of difficulty. The difference is the crater of despair the pain creates.

For many, the agony is so great that they wake up each morning wondering how they will possibly make it through another day. Sadly, some don't and take their own lives. Others die a different death; while they don't forfeit their bodies, they do relinquish everything else that makes them human and simply shrivel up to the point where family members no longer recognize them. The intricacies that made them unique and special have evaporated along with their peace and joy. They are simply a shell of their former selves and are completely hollow inside. They have died a spiritual and emotional death.

Many choose to cope through drug use, whether the "drug" is sex, food, alcohol, cocaine, sleep, or relationships. Whatever the hypnotic, when used illicitly or excessively— that is, outside of God's intent—it is employed to inhibit reality. It anesthetizes the user's existence, deadening the world around them just as novocaine deadens nerve tissue. However, novocaine aids in fixing an ailment; drugs are used to avoid one. It inhibits not just exposure to the pain but also the solution to fix it.

"Users" know that it's not solving their problems. In fact, most would confess that it further exasperates them. Why in the world would they continue using then? From an outside perspective, it makes no sense. Why would they continue to do something that they know will only bring greater suffering?

In many cases, it's all that separates them from insanity or death. These individuals have little hope of ever finding peace because each attempt is accompanied by greater despair. All they find is more void. Just when they think they've hit rock bottom, a trap door opens and they descend another ten feet. Believing they have exhausted every conceivable remedy for their despair, they give up and settle for being sedated. They are simply surviving.

This is the exact situation Mindy found her father in a couple of years ago. She writes:

> "Is there no balm in Gilead? Is there no physician there?" (Jeremiah 8:22). This was my cry. Little did I know that in the midst of my seemingly crumbling life, God was at work. Yes, there is a balm in Gilead. There is a physician there. And His name is

Jehovah-rophe, the Lord who heals. I came to know the Lord by this name through an experience I will never forget.

It began right after my dad made the decision to pull out of a business partnership in obedience to Scripture and enroll our family into a Bible-based education program. A spiritual attack began that was beyond anything we had ever experienced. Our family went through a major struggle when one in our family experienced deep depression. I had never understood depression before. I always thought that if the person would only "get a grip," they could overcome their hopelessness. I now understand that it runs much deeper.

It was hard to see one of my own with no fight nor energy left within him, and his strength dried up like clay. Seeing him wanting to end his life was like a sharp arrow in my heart. There were times I would question God's hand on us at all. Did He hear my prayers? Did He care?

Thankfully, the story doesn't end here. But before we get to it, some additional groundwork needs to be laid.

Torrential Rains

We all face adverse times, some of which undoubtedly test, if not hinder, our walk with Christ. What determines whether we come away from such storms strengthened or deflated, encouraged or bewildered? Why do trials produce hope in some and despair in others? Is there one variable that we could point to and with high probability predict where people fall?

Perhaps one clue in understanding the variance in reactions is the shelter that is sought when the storm hits. Whether God causes or permits affliction, how we frame the purpose behind it will, in part, determine the shelter we seek. If we see none or attribute it to an uncaring or perhaps handcuffed God, we begin to seek our own means in trying to rectify the situation.

Blaming God is an extremely convenient strategy. It affords us the opportunity to deflect responsibility, exonerating ourselves from any role our sin may have played in the current suffering. After all, God is the one who has become cold and distant. God is the one who has become unresponsive, making it that much easier to place ourselves back on the throne. If He isn't going to act, I will.

If this is you, it would be prudent to recheck your coordinates. You are correct. A gap has developed. It is real. However, the question is, who moved? If you chart your position and compare it to where you were before the misery (not the pain) began, you will notice that God didn't move, you did. God loves you and wants only the best for you. He told a tired Moses, "Be strong and courageous, do not be afraid or tremble at them [enemy nations], for the Lord your God is the one who goes with you. He will not fail you or forsake you" (Deuteronomy 31:6). God makes the same promise to you today. As Mindy so succinctly states later on in her letter, "God always meets us at the point of our obedience." What a powerful sentence!

It's important to understand that pain serves a purpose. God uses it, at times, to warn us that something is wrong and that action is required. It's instructional in nature. Either you alter course and address the affliction, or you simply ignore it and continue down the same deadly path. A man who suddenly experiences radiating chest discomfort has a choice to make. If he chooses to ignore the pain and continues walking, he risks dying. He is having a heart attack; the muscle is not receiving adequate oxygen due to a closing artery. If the channel that delivers the life-sustaining blood is not stinted, the heart muscle will die and so will he. The cause of death is oxygen deprivation. It would be foolish to not seek a physician's assistance when there is still time to act.

Yet this is exactly what we do when a parallel event happens to our spiritual hearts. Rather than seek the Physician's assistance and stint the closing vessel, we choose to continue walking. In doing so, we slowly but methodically starve our cells of the nutrients required to live abundantly. When we are no longer fed by the only One who can truly sustain us, we die spiritually. The cause of this death is mercy deprivation.

While pain may be part of God's design, despair is not. It is a consequence of placing ourselves on the throne when the pain surfaces. While we should take advantage of the opportunity to grow our faith, we instead use it as an excuse to abandon that faith. Consequently, we pay a price. Leaning on God and suffering from hopelessness are inversely correlated. As one goes down, the other goes up. As our level of trust in God drops, the level of despair we feel elevates. Consequently, we rob Him of the glory and ourselves of joy. We cut ourselves off from the very source that will assist in addressing the pain that we're fleeing.

But don't rely on me. Perform your own assessment and see if my hypothesis is true. Walk through your past and pinpoint the lows (despair, hopelessness) and then dissect your relationship with God during that period. Did the pattern emerge?

Monotonous Drips

As you're reading this, you may be unable to recall one particular turning point that led to the despair. You simply woke up one day and realized that things weren't good. The process of dethroning God and the despair that follows is not always due to some great traumatic storm(s). It could very well be the result of repetitive, benign-appearing sin, like water dripping on a rock. The impact of one drop has no appreciable impact. Over the course of many years and hundreds of thousands of drops later, however, its cumulative damage begins to reveal itself via a cavity.

I was inadvertently reminded of this during a conversation my wife and I had with her friend, Jessica. She was relating her experiences working as a nanny in Boston a few years ago. She and some fellow nannies would go to the market and buy live lobster. They would then return home and race them across the kitchen floor. The lobster that came in last would get boiled first.

Joking about the game's barbaric nature, I commented that an alternative would be to simply place the lobster in water at room temperature and then slowly turn up the heat. Oblivious to the gradual increase, the lobster would be inconspicuously ushered into death. There would be no fight.

With quiet passion, Jessica made an eloquent parallel to our spiritual walk. For some, the jarring event of being dumped into the proverbial boiling water elicits a sharp reaction to fight just as it does in the lobster. Rather than destroy our walk, it triggers a rededication. The events that appear mundane may be the real danger. Just as the lobster was lulled into death by events that appeared benign, the same can happen to us in our walk with God. Paul warns us of such dangers when he writes, "But I am afraid, lest as the serpent deceived Eve by his craftiness, your minds should be led astray from the simplicity and purity of devotion to Christ" (2 Corinthians 11:3). Before we know it, we wake up one day wondering how things got so bad.

Regardless of whether the distance between you and God was due to some jarring event or long-standing inattentiveness, the despair you feel is unnecessary and not part of

God's plan for you and your life. To the extent that you continue pulling away from Him and rely upon yourself for understanding, you not only sustain the despair, you will further fuel it. Until you realize that the shelter you seek is nothing more than a shack held together by rotted boards and rusty nails, every storm that hits will leave you trembling and soaking wet.

Picking up Mindy's story where we left off:

I had many opportunities to become bitter at God, yet thankfully He lovingly showed me in His Word a better way.

Exodus 15:22-27 gives us the account where Moses led Israel into the wilderness of Shur, where they spent three days without finding water. (Do you think Moses took a wrong turn? No—God had them right where He wanted them. I believe God had our family right where He wanted us, too.) When they came to the waters of Marah, they realized they could not drink, for the waters were bitter. In the same way, that is exactly what bitterness does to a person; it makes us useless and no good to others. I didn't want to become useless like the bitter waters of Marah. I wanted to be useful. I knew then that becoming bitter toward God or toward the one going through this depression was not an option.

"What shall we drink?" the Israelites grumbled at Moses because of the bitter waters. Moses then cried out to the Lord for an answer. I think this is very significant. Many times when faced with a difficult situation, where do we turn? Isn't it usually to other people? Where we turn for help could make the difference between life and death, physically and/or spiritually. It could also make the difference between oppression (bondage) and peace (freedom). Whether an illness is physical, emotional, or spiritual, a person should first seek healing from Jehovah-rophe. Second Chronicles 16:12 states, "And in the thirty-ninth year of his reign Asa became diseased in his feet. His disease was severe, yet even in his disease he did not seek the Lord but the physicians." God may, and often does, use physicians and others as His instruments of healing. Yet, ultimately, the instrument is powerless without the Physician's power.

God heard the prayer of Moses and answered him. God told him to cast a tree into the water. When Moses obeyed the voice of the Lord, the waters were made sweet! **God always meets us at the point of our obedience.** I believe sweet healing came to our family because we sought our Jehovah-rophe—the Lord who heals. He is the one that lifted us up. He is the one that healed the troubled mind of our loved one. Out of our suffering came a wonderful thing—He gave us a song to sing! A family unity developed that was closer than it had ever been. As a result, we joined together and to this day, we are worshiping our Jehovah-rophe in song. We have much to rejoice in! There is power in His name!

As Moses applied the tree to the waters, they became sweet. As you and I apply the cross (Calvary's tree) to the bitter waters of our life, we will be made whole. Only one Physician can heal the ills of our souls. Why look elsewhere? "Who is among you that fears the Lord, that obeys the voice of His servant, that walks in darkness and has no light? Let him trust in the name of the Lord and rely on his God" (Isaiah 50:10).

Do you have bitter waters that need sweetening? Run to Jehovah-rophe. He is waiting to show Himself strong to you, to make your life sweet, and to give you a new song to sing![3]

In 2 Corinthians, Paul provides the biblical foundation for maintaining hope:

> But in everything commending ourselves as servants of God, in much endurance, in afflictions, in hardships, in distresses, in beatings, in imprisonments, in tumults, in labors, in sleeplessness, in hunger, in purity, in knowledge, in patience, in kindness, in the Holy Spirit, in genuine love, in the word of truth, in the power of God; by the weapons of righteousness for the right hand and the left, by glory and dishonor, by evil report and good report; regarded as deceivers and yet true; as unknown yet well-known, as dying yet behold, we live; as punished yet not put to death, as sorrowful yet always rejoicing, as poor yet making many rich, as having nothing yet possessing all things (6:4-10).

Run to the pain rather than from it. In doing so, you will find in the epicenter of the storm the only true shelter—God Himself. It's time to pack up and move, taking cover in the Lord's house.

2

Jesus—Our Deliverer

The passage from 2 Corinthians with which I closed the last chapter speaks of peace regardless of circumstance. I would have scoffed at the notion a relatively short time ago. Was Paul deranged when he wrote the verses? You may be thinking as I did, "Surely they don't apply to my life." After all, Paul would recant some of the language if he only knew your circumstances, right?

Wrong. God inspired the verses. They are as relevant and applicable today as they were when the Apostle wrote them some twenty years after Christ's crucifixion. Paul is writing from personal experience. If the passage held water for a man who not only called himself the chief of sinners but also suffered from intense persecution, it's plausible that it could work for you, too.

As the book's title proclaims, our only hope of finding joy, regardless of the situation, is faith in Jesus Christ, our Deliverer: He will safely deliver you *to* the Father's house and *from* misery.

In his book *Reaching for the Invisible God*, Philip

Yancey explains, "Faith can survive periods of darkness but only if we cling to it in the midst of the darkness."[4] He writes from personal experience, not as a removed third party relying upon the accounts of others to explain that which he has not faced. He has grappled with many of the same questions that currently haunt you. And without equivocation, he finds himself coming back to the same answer over and over—Christ.

At my father's church recently, the congregation sang a hymn that most of us have turned to a hundred times, *What a Friend We Have in Jesus.* I wonder, though, how many times we have actually meditated over the words and allowed them to penetrate our souls. Is this the Jesus you see? Is He your refuge? Joseph Scriven wrote the lyrics in 1855 to console a lonely and heartbroken mother living on the other side of the Atlantic in Ireland.

> What a Friend we have in Jesus, all our sins and griefs to bear!
> What a privilege to carry everything to God in prayer!
> O what peace we often forfeit, O what needless pain we bear,
> All because we do not carry everything to God in prayer.
>
> Have we trials and temptations? Is there trouble anywhere?
> We should never be discouraged; take it to the Lord in prayer.
> Can we find a friend so faithful who will all our sorrows share?
> Jesus knows our every weakness; take it to the Lord in prayer.

> Are we weak and heavy laden, cumbered with a load of care?
> Precious Savior, still our refuge, take it to the Lord in prayer.
> Do your friends despise, forsake you? Take it to the Lord in prayer!
> In His arms He'll take and shield you; you will find a solace there.[5]

There is a place to take our concerns. We don't have to wrestle with them on our own. We have Jesus! He is not some distant deity completely removed from the cares of those He rules over; Christ understands what trial is. God took on human flesh and for thirty-three years endured the greatest wave of carnality man could muster. Jesus knows pain. He experienced hatred, temptation, mockery, torture, betrayal, ignorance, and ridicule. But unlike a caring friend who can only listen and empathize, Christ is empowered to remove the agony of those burdens and give you a hope despite them. All you need to do is ASK through prayer!

Traveling through central Missouri on our way from Kansas City to St. Louis one summer, my wife and I decided to take a more scenic, less traveled path. As we navigated from one small town to another, we ran across not only beautiful terrain but also numerous churches. One in particular caught my eye. It was called the Church of Hope. Beneath the name it aptly read, "Jesus is our only hope." It is a simple sentence—only five words. But the freedom one can gain by embracing its significance is overwhelming. "It was for freedom that Christ set us free; therefore keep standing firm and do not be subject again to a yoke of slavery" (Galatians 5:1). Contrary to conventional wisdom, an oxymoron in and of itself, Jesus Christ is not the chain; He is the chain breaker.

It's a glory I try to capture metaphorically throughout

this book. Association is a powerful literary device. It allows a writer to explain that which hasn't been fully experienced by linking it to something that has. In the context of showing Christ, I knew I could achieve but partial elucidation. The English language, even with its plethora of superlatives, is simply ill-equipped to get its arms around the complete Christ and the supreme joy that can be known through Him. You will never grasp the full gravity of His glory by merely reading about it.

It would be like trying to convey through story and illustration the flavor of a fudge sundae to a child who has never tried ice cream before. Oh, one could describe the physical characteristics, but not that which creates the actual craving—its irresistible sweetness. It isn't until you dive in and taste that first spoonful that the true love affair begins. The same goes for Jesus: Christ did not die on the cross merely to be explained but so that we might experience Him in the most direct and personal manner possible. Only then will you understand the ineffable pleasure He offers.

Because of Jesus, we can fulfill God's commandment to delight in Him. For some of you, this may seem impossible right now. Following Christ and seeking your fulfillment in Him alone may appear to present unsurpassable perils. I encourage you to take a leap of faith and make yourself vulnerable to Him. Remove yourself from denominational labels for they mean absolutely nothing if your savior is a mere hollow cavity. Make a connection with the true Savior and yearn for Him and His Word like a child craves her mother's milk (1 Peter 2:2-3).[6] He will satisfy your hunger pangs for joy and peace. You will not be left unfed.

Part II

Meeting Us at the Point of Our Obedience

Below are stories of individuals who availed themselves of God's great glory by simply giving Christ His due—their hearts. The Lord met their acts of faith in a powerful manner that far exceeded expectation.

Though they appear sensational, each one of these testimonies is true. Collectively, they point to a caring, loving Savior who will meet us at the point of our obedience. I pray that these accounts will challenge as well as encourage you.

3

Taking Out the Garbage

Chuck Raichert loves Jesus Christ, and it shows. He radiates a joy that is contagious. You don't have to be in his presence long to realize that he is at peace. This hasn't always been the case, however.

The road Chuck traveled prior to accepting Christ as Savior was bumpy to state it mildly. It was marked with roadblocks, detours, and potholes. If ever there was a person who could have used a copy of this book, it was Chuck Raichert himself thirty years ago. He was the epitome of hopelessness and despair. Outlined below is his story; it's a testimony to God's tremendous grace and sovereignty.

Chuck grew up in a home in which family members didn't know the Lord and were unable to express love to one another. Chuck was constantly told that he wouldn't amount to anything. In fact, one of his father's favorite phrases was, "Your brother received artistic skills, your sister a keen intellect, but there was nothing left over for you in the gene pool." His parents' expectations low, Chuck did his best not to disappoint.

Believing he was unlovable and unworthy, he spent the first twenty-five years of his life searching for acceptance while trying to escape the pain that accompanied not finding it. Unfortunately, he was, as the famous song goes, looking for love in all the wrong places. At each juncture, there was initial relief, but it was quickly followed by a greater severity of emptiness. The more he sought happiness, the worse his life became.

It began with alcohol. He was eleven years old the first time he got drunk. By age fourteen, he was drinking regularly. He and his buddies would stop at the neighborhood grocery store and steal whatever they needed for that night's escape.

When the alcohol no longer satisfied him, he added drugs to the equation. He was only sixteen years old. He started with pot and worked his way up to cocaine, LSD, and opium. Each progression represented a renewed attempt to fill the hole in his heart.

Needing to support his increasingly expensive habits, Chuck started selling when he was a senior in high school. And he did quite well; there was never less than $1,000 in his cookie jar. The cops would be sitting out front scoping his house; he would be in back carrying out a transaction. To this day, Chuck is amazed that he was never arrested and convicted.

Over the next seven years, he lost four of his friends to drug overdose. A gang member killed a fifth because he and Chuck were underpricing the market by selling drugs at lower cost. Chuck himself carried a Colt 45 because he constantly feared for his life.

The lifestyle began taking a physical toll on Chuck. By the mid 1970s, after ten years of heavy use, he had become a skeleton of his former self. He had lost close to fifty pounds and was too weak even to walk up a flight of stairs.

Chuck Raichert should have died. He had abused his

body for a long time engaging in the same activities that killed many of his friends.

And he wanted to die. In his mind, he had two choices: end the earthly misery then and there by taking his own life, or continue the drug use at his current pace and wait for his organs to shut down. Not great options. Though Chuck seriously considered suicide, his fear of hell prevented him from following through. Even though he was certain that it was his ultimate destination, there was no reason to expedite the process. Simply staying high and waiting to die would have to suffice.

Chuck correctly believed that there was a hell. What he misunderstood was how to avoid it. That was about to change, however.

Chuck came to a crossroads. It was January of 1976, and he had just overdosed for the third time. The doctor made it clear that if it happened again, he wouldn't survive. Due to the prayers of his wife Polly and his recognition of the fact that death and hell were now only one good snort away, he became more receptive to the Gospel message. Clearly, God had begun pricking his heart.

As far back as he could remember, Chuck had operated under the assumption that he was unworthy and unlovable, particularly in relation to God. He was half right. He is unworthy, as is the entire fallen race. We all fall short of the Lord's standard. But he is lovable if the source of that love is a God who is capable of dispensing it unconditionally. And the God of the Bible is. Chuck failed to understand this.

He concluded that God's love, like man's, is earned. Thankfully, it is not. If it were, we would all be destined for hell. He chooses to seek us despite our faults and shortcomings. This is grace. God loves us even when He has every reason to do the opposite. As Yancey so succinctly states, "Grace, like water, flows to the lowest part."[7]

The clearest demonstration of this love was the provision

of an escape hatch from hell—namely, His Son, Jesus Christ. It is a free gift. All we are asked to do is surrender to the Savior. Raised in a home where performance drove acceptance, Chuck was unwilling or perhaps unable to accept the concept. Given his upbringing, escapism in the face of the reality around him seemed, if not logical, at least understandable. Fortunately for us, Chuck's was an errant theology. We should be joyful that God doesn't dispense His mercy commensurate with our ability to earn it, for if He did, our existence would be dark.

The weight of this tremendous truth began to penetrate Chuck's soul. With his wife's encouragement, he realized that he needed to make a decision. Continuing with the status quo was no longer an option. He was sitting on the floor in his duplex in northeast Minneapolis with his two infant sons when he cried out to the Lord, "If you are real, please come into my life." Chuck Raichert had just invited Jesus Christ into his heart as his Lord and Savior.

It was truly a miracle. Chuck's debt was now paid in full by the blood of Jesus. The burden of the past had been lifted. The hope and acceptance he had long sought were now his. He immediately stopped drinking and taking drugs, as there was no reason to continue numbing himself from reality; he had finally found a solution to fill that huge hole in his heart. Unlike his other attempts to find sustainable peace, this one was not temporal and hollow but permanent and complete.

Admittedly, it was a bit scary. The unfamiliar usually is, particularly when it's of supernatural origin. He nonetheless forged ahead and began attending his wife's church. While somewhat intimidated, he could see that God was real and trustworthy. To publicly testify to his newfound faith, he was baptized in 1977.

Sensing he had a special gift, some members of the congregation asked Chuck to think about entering the ministry. After picking himself up off the floor, he responded,

"Who me? You don't know my past. How could God possibly use me?" That's the amazing power of the resurrection—it offers the chance to wipe the slate clean. Chuck quickly realized that God had granted him a fresh start. What a joy it was that the baggage of the past was just that. It had been left at the feet of Jesus. He no longer had to look backwards; he could now focus on the future.

In 1978, led by the Lord, he became a deacon in the church. A year later, he accepted the assistant pastorship.

Thanks to the encouragement of the senior pastor, John Bronner, he decided in 1980 to attend Northwestern Bible College. He began preparing for senior leadership ministry. Though he could barely read even comic strips when he first entered, Chuck worked hard at his studies. He was able to successfully complete two years of school and became licensed. When John passed away in 1982, Chuck became the church's interim pastor.

Eager to demonstrate that he was worthy of God's calling, Chuck set out on a rapid pace. He had great energy. There was only one problem. He left out of the equation the One who blessed him with the opportunity in the first place—Jesus. Chuck was more concerned with *appearing* spiritual than *being* spiritual. He busied himself with work that outwardly looked biblical in order to impress. Reputation, not God, drove his actions. He was robbing Christ of the glory, hoarding it all for himself.

The pinnacle of this carnality came when he was performing a wedding he knew God did not condone. Because Chuck wanted to impress his family with his great spiritual leadership, he ignored warnings and performed the ceremony anyway. There was no way he was going to pass up this opportunity to perform. As Chuck quickly learned, God condemns the proud.

Guilt came showering down as Chuck began to comprehend what he had done. This was his first real test as a

Christian. Would it grow his faith or hamper it? Would he take his burden to the cross or seek his own means? Immature in his walk and susceptible to outside attack, he regrettably did the latter and began buying into Satan's lies. Reverting back to his "old theology" according to which performance determined acceptance, Chuck concluded that he had irreversibly failed God. There was no hope of reconciling what he had done. The damage was too great.

With his guard down, he watched things go from bad to worse. Sin cornered his life, and he quickly found himself in an immoral relationship. It is amazing how fast and how far we fall when we brush God aside. Ashamed, defeated, and deceived, he continued his folly. Chuck left home and moved in with the woman.

It was a horrific four-month period. He had completely lost the hope and peace he once knew. And the hole in his heart reemerged. The all-too-familiar stench of sin once again filled his nostrils. Chuck hated his transgressions because he knew they hurt God (a sign that reinforced for him that he was truly saved). Nonetheless, the garbage his wickedness produced was piling up and beginning to rot.

Deep down he knew that there was only one way to remove the odor. Clearly, continuing a relationship with the woman wasn't the answer. Christ was the only plausible solution. The question was whether the Lord would be willing to take him back and pluck this sinner, once again, from the jaws of hopelessness.

Drawn back to Scripture, he found a small remnant of hope. Perhaps inner peace would be possible once more. Time would tell. Even though he saw no hope of reconciliation between his wife and him, he assembled enough obedience to end the promiscuity and return home to his family.

Chuck was stunned at what awaited him. He expected to find a wife in great distress, but he didn't. Polly had peace. While his own spiritual life had withered, hers had blossomed. She had taken the agony of the separation and given it to Christ to bear. Her joy was now dependent upon the Lord, not Chuck. This newfound freedom came from attending Rebuilder Ministries, an organization started by John Hartzell. She learned that Christ is the true source of all joy. Unlike man, He would never leave or forsake her. With new and fresh understanding, she had every reason to be hopeful.

One thing was sure. The control he wielded over his wife and her happiness these many years was gone. Chuck had involuntarily relinquished it. A force far more powerful had crumbled his reign. He was, quite simply, dethroned by the King of kings Himself. It was a huge blow to Chuck's ego, and he became extremely angry. He considered Polly's newfound freedom a usurpation of her need for him. And to a certain degree, it was. Polly still loved Chuck and desired to have a caring, loving relationship with him, but if that didn't happen, she would be sad but not devastated.

Over the next few months, Chuck found this envy for power taking on new form. While still angry about being "dethroned," he slowly became more curious and even a bit jealous of Polly's contentment. Though he didn't admit to it at the time, Chuck began desiring what his wife had in Christ.

It's an interesting dynamic. He was fighting to retain control yet yearned for the freedom that results from relinquishing it. Realizing that the two impulses could not coexist, he, too, eventually recognized the need for a transfer of power. Though it would take him a good year after returning home to make the leap of faith, he began joining Polly at Rebuilders. There he found help in handing over the reins. It was, in hindsight, the first step in what has been a fruitful and prosperous journey.

Throughout the next two years, Chuck worked aggressively to restore his marriage with Polly as well as his relationship with the Lord. While the transition was not always smooth, he found that God was faithful and kept His promises.

Feeling refreshed and ready to serve, he communicated his desire to return to ministry. Mary Hartzell, John's wife, quickly but lovingly admonished Chuck. She made it clear that he needed to wait and lean on the Lord, lest he repeat the patterns of the past. He heeded her advice. It wasn't until 1986, after three years under John's teaching at Rebuilders, that he began to play a more formal role. He went from leading music to eventually teaching. With each step, Chuck waited and leaned.

Wanting to reach out and tell his story, Chuck began meeting one-on-one with others who were struggling. It was the beginning of what today is a more formal counseling ministry. His goal was to show Christ and the joy that comes from personally knowing Him. Chuck was in a somewhat unique position. Not only could he relate to their despair; he was also living proof that there was an alternative. Bondage did not have to be their destiny. Christ could set them free.

Anyone who has ever visited Chuck's office has noticed a wooden plaque engraved with Hebrews 12:2: "Fixing our eyes on Jesus, the author and perfecter of faith, who for the joy set before Him endured the cross, despising the shame, and has sat down at the right hand of the throne of God." This verse is all about liberty—liberty in Christ. Our task is simply to look for it. There's a reason for its position right above his desk: the verse serves as a daily reminder that if we fix our eyes on anything other than Him, despair will come knocking.

In 1988, John Hartzell accepted the position of senior pastor at Normandale Baptist Church in Bloomington, Minnesota. Feeling called to full-time ministry and eager to follow his mentor, Chuck became the church's Rebuilders pastor. He brought with him the same passion and drive to see people experience the true Christ.

Over these many years, Chuck has ministered to hundreds of people, helping them realize the power of biblical reconciliation. He is absolutely amazed at what God can do with a person who is willing to yield control and lean upon Him for their every step.

In May of 2002, John retired, and Chuck became senior pastor. Though busy with the daily responsibilities of leading a church, he continues to counsel.

Chuck and Polly are today deeply in love and best friends. They are enjoying the fruits of placing Jesus on the throne. In June of 2003, they celebrated their 31st anniversary. In recalling the roller coaster ride of the previous three decades, Polly shared that she stands in awe of her God's mercy and faithfulness. He has brought a joy and peace into their marriage that seemed impossible when Chuck first returned home in 1982. When Jesus is leading the way, no differences are irreconcilable. Chuck and Polly are living testimonies to this truth.

Today, the Raicherts have eight children and three grandchildren. A side note: I thought it was worth print to share one quick fact about them. Chuck and Polly's oldest son is a Minneapolis police officer and their second oldest a Hennepin County deputy sheriff. Considering Chuck's interesting past, I found this somewhat ironical. We worship a God with a great sense of humor.

I have outlined Chuck's path not to glorify his sin but to illustrate two lessons: one, as bad as it may seem, there is always hope in Christ; and two, regardless of your past, God can and will use you in miraculous ways moving forward. Where the repentant sinner is concerned, there is no such thing as "damaged goods" in His eyes. God took one particular man who was joyless and completely beaten and delivered him *twice* from the pit of despair.

Do you have a lot of garbage piled up? It matters not how high the pile or how offensive the odor. Let Christ dispose of it.

4

Securing True Love

For all intents and purposes, Henry and Liz led separate lives. They not only slept apart but also lived in separate sections of the house: he in the basement and she upstairs. They never spoke or touched. Their means of communication consisted of writing notes and placing them in strategic locations so that the other would stumble upon them.

Even though they were both Christians, their relationship had become nothing more than a barely tolerable coexistence. In thirty years of marriage, they had accumulated so much bitterness towards each other that it had festered into pure hatred. Their arrangement more closely resembled a prison sentence than a union joined by God.

As is the case with most torn relationships, sin was the wedge that drove them apart. Henry was a cross-dresser. Liz had her suspicions but was unable to confirm them. What was readily apparent was that a blanket of transgression had shrouded the relationship. It was suffocating both of them.

Things came to a head when their daughter pulled into the driveway one day. As she was opening the garage door, there was Henry decked out in women's clothing. Completely disgusted, Liz kicked him out of the house and had a restraining order placed on him. She was done with the marriage.

Henry was shocked by what he considered Liz's overreaction. How harmful could dressing as a woman be? It wasn't hurting anyone. Nevertheless, with divorce facing him squarely in the eye, he was stunned into the realization that the issue was enormously destructive and needed to be addressed immediately.

To Henry's credit, he took the initiative of contacting his church counselor. Never having seen this particular situation before and believing deep down it was hopeless anyhow, the counselor called Chuck. She had heard of him through a colleague and figured it couldn't hurt. She asked if he had ever dealt with cross-dressing. He had and was more than happy to meet with Henry if he was willing. Embarrassed and increasingly desperate, Henry did accept the invitation.

Chuck's first task was to help Henry see his "problem" as sin. Until this point, he had blamed his wife and mother for his behavior. Henry had had a poor relationship with both women. They were the ones who, by not loving him in a manner he found acceptable, created the void in the first place. His cross-dressing, he rationalized, was simply an attempt to fill that gap. It gave him a sense that he was loved.

The only source of true, unadulterated love, however, is Christ, Chuck explained. Until Henry understood this, his desire to seek alternatives would continue to devour him. Chuck navigated him through 1 Corinthians 6:18-20:

> Flee immorality. Every other sin that a man commits is outside the body, but the immoral man sins against his own body. Or do you not know that your body is a temple of the Holy Spirit who is in you, whom you

have from God, and that you are not your own? For you have been bought with a price: therefore glorify God in your body.

He also had Henry focus on 1 Thessalonians 4:3-8:

For this is the will of God, your sanctification; that is, that you abstain from sexual immorality; that each of you know how to possess his own vessel in sanctification and honor, not in lustful passion, like the Gentiles who do not know God; and that no man transgress and defraud his brother in the matter because the Lord is the avenger in all these things, just as we also told you before and solemnly warned you. For God has not called us for the purpose of impurity, but in sanctification. Consequently, he who rejects this is not rejecting man but the God who gives His Holy Spirit to you.

While it took time, Henry did eventually become convicted. He realized that his sin, not his wife or mother, was the source of the problem. It was time to take his transgression and the despair it caused to the cross.

A gentleman attending a recent Rebuilders meeting commented that faith and fear (unbiblical fear) cannot coexist. The same principle applies to faith and despair. One precludes the other. The key is determining which one will receive the power to rule. You cannot serve two masters. It's either God or self. Henry chose God.

During the next month, Chuck saw amazing progress in this man. The sin that kept him from communing with his Lord had vanished. In Christ, Henry found a reservoir of true love and no longer needed women's clothes. In fact, he threw them in the trash. As an accountability measure, Henry gave a church elder twenty-four hour access to his apartment to ensure that he wasn't reverting back to his old ways.

He was a changed person and looked forward to eventually moving home. He had restored his vertical relationship with God and now needed to work on his horizontal one with Liz in order to complete the cross.

Having heard that Henry was doing better, Liz called Chuck. Despite his progress, she felt that her husband still needed professional help. Chuck conveyed to her that Henry had been receiving such care. Intrigued but somewhat skeptical, she countered, "Oh, you are a professional?" Chuck replied, "No, but I am employed by One who is." Although Liz was not completely amused, Chuck's response did help take the edge off, and she agreed to meet him in person. This was something Liz had been, up until now, unwilling to do.

They sat down together on a Thursday night. Liz was defensive and determined to blame Henry for all the problems within the marriage. Nonetheless, Chuck gently turned the conversation back toward her. There was nothing she could do to change her husband. That was the Lord's work. Liz's focus, he emphasized, needed to be on her own walk with God.

As he had done with Henry, Chuck walked her through Scripture. He started with 1 Peter 3:1-4:

> In the same way, you wives, be submissive to your own husbands so that even if any of them are disobedient to the word, they may be won without a word by the behavior of their wives, as they observe your chaste and respectful behavior. And let not your adornment be external only—braiding the hair, and wearing gold jewelry, and putting on dresses; but let it be the hidden person of the heart, with the imperishable quality of a gentle and quiet spirit, which is precious in the sight of God.

Chuck explained that in Christ we become different people. As Paul asserts in Colossians, we put aside some things and put on others:

> But now you also, put them all aside: anger, wrath, malice, slander, and abusive speech from your mouth. Do not lie to one another, since you laid aside the old self with its evil practices, and have put on the new self who is being renewed to a true knowledge according to the image of the One who created him (3:8-10).

> And so, as those who have been chosen of God, holy and beloved, put on a heart of compassion, kindness, humility, gentleness, and patience; bearing with one another, and forgiving each other, whoever has a complaint against any one; just as the Lord forgave you, so also should you. And beyond all these things put on love, which is the perfect bond of unity. And let the peace of Christ rule in your hearts, to which indeed you were called in one body; and be thankful (3:12-15).

Though Liz had read these passages before, they were now touching her as never before. A new understanding of her Lord and His design for her life began to surface. She realized that divorcing her husband was not an option. She embraced 1 Corinthians 7:10: "But to the married I give instructions, not I, but the Lord, that the wife should not leave her husband."

By the time they finished their conversation some two hours later, a huge weight had been lifted from Liz's shoulders. She didn't need to bear the burden of her marriage. She simply needed to hand it over to her Lord and avail herself of the peace only He can offer. It was time to forgive and be forgiven.

The following Monday, Chuck received a phone call. It was the church's counselor again. She was calling with mixed emotions. Henry had been reinstated (he had been restricted from holding a position within the church until he had repented of his sin) and had ushered on Sunday morning.

Of particular significance, the counselor continued, was what took place when Henry was assisting with the offertory. As he was passing his wife's pew, she unexpectedly grabbed his arm. In complete shock, he turned towards her and they spontaneously embraced. Everyone was stunned. This was a couple that never touched and didn't even sit in the same pew during the church service. The timing was remarkable. That evening, Henry had a massive heart attack and died.

In speaking with Chuck at the funeral, Liz explained to him that while mournful of the loss, she did have peace. The two had reconciled during their embrace Sunday morning. In the nick of time, they had each taken their deep-seated anger towards the other and released it to the Lord. They gave Him the reins. Christ tore down and discarded, in a moment's notice, thirty years of barrier. That's supernatural power!

The story doesn't end there, however.

Roughly three years later, John Hartzell was attending the funeral of a family member. A couple he knew well approached him after the interment. They were having marital problems and wondered whether he had a moment to speak. As they moved to a more private location, John turned toward the couple to begin addressing their concerns. As he did, staring him straight in the eye was Henry's headstone. While John knew he had been buried somewhere in the cemetery, he had no idea where. In awe of God's great timing, John, who was very familiar with the story, gave Henry's testimony.

Rather than wait for a response from the couple, John

left them alone with their thoughts. They just stood there in front of Henry's grave trying to absorb the enormity of what was just shared. "'O DEATH, WHERE IS YOUR VICTORY? O DEATH, WHERE IS YOUR STING?' The sting of death is sin, and the power of sin is the law; but thanks be to God, who gives us the victory through our Lord Jesus Christ" (1 Corinthians 15:55-57).

Prior to seeing Chuck, everyone considered Henry and Liz's situation utterly hopeless, including Henry and Liz. He would never stop cross-dressing, they thought. She would never forgive him if he did anyhow. They would never love again. Unfortunately, we have conditioned ourselves into believing that the Bible is sufficient for salvation but not sanctification. We turn to the world and its psychology for the really big problems. And once again, we stand corrected. What is impossible for man is not only possible with Christ, but probable. Henry died a free and truly loved man.

Do you feel unlovable? If you are like Henry, it's critical to understand that the very Author of love—God—dispenses it unconditionally. The One who created you and knows your every thought wants you to experience His affections in great abundance. Take a few minutes and camp on that thought. Let its significance sink in and penetrate your soul. It's a glorious truth that should leave you in awe!

Remember, God created us that we may glorify Him. He receives no honor when you feel unloved. It's not part of His design. Unlike your ties with man, your standing with Him is not provisional. While sin may damage the relationship and halt blessing, it does not prevent God from caring for you. If you have concluded that He no longer does, it is because you have bought into Satan's deception.

Turn from these lies and stand in awe of the unparalleled sweetness of God's love.

5

Forfeit to Win

Born into a Catholic family in 1947, Pete was taught that salvation was contingent upon two things: being baptized as an infant and following all the rules and regulations of the Church. Noncompliance would mean, for the more serious sins, spending eternity in hell; the lesser transgressions would be punished temporarily in purgatory. While it was impressed upon him that Jesus rose from the dead, the fact that He died a substitutive death so that Pete might be justified in God's eyes was left untouched.

Home life was difficult. Pete's father, Bill, was a traveling salesman. Because he was seldom around, his mother was forced to raise the family alone. The long periods of separation weren't necessarily bad, however. For when he was home, life became exponentially more arduous. Bill was a very angry man and had a fierce temper. Being an ex-marine, he believed in harsh discipline. The children did their best to stay out of his path, particularly Pete.

Not surprisingly, his parents had a strained marriage; it was wrought with pain. They fought constantly. The one small gem hidden amidst all the disarray, however, was the fact that, regardless of how bad things got, they never considered divorce an option. This reality had a profound impact on Pete and would help shape his thinking on the issue later in life.

Understandably, Pete's tough upbringing had a detrimental impact on him. He was constantly in trouble as a teenager and had many run-ins with the law. Not sure what to do with him, his parents shipped him first to a reformatory school and then to a military boarding institution. The time away only caused him to become more angry and rebellious. He sought escape and relief through drinking. By the time he was a senior in high school, he had become a drunk.

Lacking any specific plans or any formal training, Pete wandered from job to job after graduating in 1965. It would take him several years to find steady employment. He met, in 1971, the girl of his dreams. She was extremely beautiful, and he fell in love with her almost immediately. Though they barely knew each other, the couple married after dating for only three weeks. Sadly, the union lasted less than a year and a half.

Pete would have other women in his life, but they existed in his eyes simply to emotionally and physically please him. It would be a stretch to characterize these relationships as loving and nurturing.

Seeking greater stability, Pete enlisted with the Marine Corps in 1976 and was stationed at Oceanside, California. He was twenty-eight and the oldest of 1,600 recruits. His drill instructors called him "Gramps." The added maturity served him well, however, as he rose quickly in rank. While excelling on base, he struggled when off. He continued to lead a promiscuous, wayward lifestyle, and it was beginning to wear on him. Though he tried repeatedly to change, Pete was unable to do so. He turned to the Catholic Church for help. But it, too, was unable to give him the answers he sought.

While he was drinking alone in a bar one night, a man sitting near him introduced himself. His name was Jim. The two men struck up a conversation. Not long into it, the stranger asked Pete out of the blue if he would like to have an abundant life. "Sure, who wouldn't?" Pete responded curiously. Jim claimed to know where to find it and invited his new friend to attend a film the following night. Thinking it couldn't hurt, he accepted.

The screening began with an introduction by the group's charismatic founder. He indicated that God had given him an insight hidden since apostolic times. The meat of his message was that you must be born again to reach heaven. The prologue was so captivating and dynamic that the film itself was a bit of a letdown and somewhat anticlimactic.

With his interest piqued, Pete agreed to go to Jim's house after the film for a fellowship gathering. There he would have the opportunity to speak with members of the organization. He was impressed. They seemed to be genuine, caring individuals. As the conversation deepened, Pete asked what had been meant by "one must be born again." They shared with him Romans 10:9: "That if you confess with your mouth Jesus as Lord, and believe in your heart that God raised Him from the dead, you shall be saved." Upon hearing this, Pete felt led to make a decision for the Lord. Jim encouraged him to pray and ask Jesus to save him. And so he did and accepted the Risen Christ right there on the spot.

Becoming more deeply involved with the organization, Pete enrolled in a thirty-two-hour session taught by the group's leader himself. This time, however, he didn't seem quite so dynamic. In fact, some of his comments seemed plain egregious. He tried to convince the class that Jesus was neither God nor virgin born. He even contended that hell didn't exist. In a moment's notice, Pete realized he had been had. This wasn't a legitimate faith-based organization. It was a cult. Rather than allow himself to be brainwashed, he made a quick exit.

While the messengers and a large portion of their message were flawed, the Christ they quoted in Romans wasn't. Thankfully, Pete was able to discern between the two and didn't rush to throw the baby out with the bath water. He had experienced a legitimate conversion. Though the events that led up to it were disturbing, for a cult is a dangerous place to be, God's sovereign message of propitiation, or atoning sacrifice, triumphed in the end. The Holy Spirit penetrated the wall of deception and laid out to Pete the Gospel unadulterated.

We worship a big God. There is no one He cannot reach. There is no circumstance He cannot penetrate. It matters not how decadent or hopeless the situation may appear. Pete's testimony is a perfect example.

It was both an exciting and somewhat scary year for Pete. He was on fire for God but had no one to disciple him. Outside of being saved, he had no clue what being a Christian actually meant. He needed guidance from other believers so that he could grow.

And God provided. Pete was informed shortly after his conversion that he was being relocated to a base in Okinawa, Japan. Upon his arrival, he learned that there was a vibrant Navigator ministry that met weekly. He made friends fast and realized how wonderful it was to be part of God's family. Pete grew tremendously in his walk. Though heavily persecuted by other marines and his commanding officer because of his faith, it was nonetheless a joyous period.

Though his spiritual life was taking off, Pete was becoming increasingly lonely and had a desire to remarry. He wasn't sure whether God would approve or not, given that he had divorced his first wife. Many of the Christians he asked thought it would be fine since the divorce occurred before he was saved. As much as he wanted to believe them, for some reason he couldn't find complete peace with their advice. He was sensing that the Holy Spirit was telling him to resist his impulse.

Confused, he took his concerns to a couple he knew well through Navigators, Tim and Chris Prater. He had been meeting with Tim for one-on-one discipleship and raised the question during one of their weekly gatherings. Tim gave Pete a pamphlet titled *Our Most Important Messages Grow Out of Our Greatest Weaknesses*.[8] He asked Pete to read it. They would discuss its contents at their next meeting.

That night, back at the barracks, Pete pored over the publication. The author made it clear that marriage is a lifelong commitment whether you are a believer or not. A vow before God is a very serious covenant; there are dire consequences in breaking it (Ecclesiastes 5:1-7). In addition, to divorce and then remarry would be considered an act of adultery (Mark 10:11-12).

After finishing it, Pete became convinced that God wanted him to remain single as long as his ex-wife was still alive. He knew his path wouldn't be easy, for it was difficult to fathom being single for the rest of his life. If he were to be obedient, Pete would need God to hold his hand at every step. He knelt down by his bed and prayed for strength.

The following week, Tim reassured Pete that God's grace was sufficient. They walked through verse after verse that demonstrated the Lord is a promise keeper. He would see him through this.

And God did.

In 1980, with his duty in the military about to end, the Navigators asked Pete if he would consider joining their staff. They needed someone to serve a two-year stint at their conference center in Colorado Springs. After much prayer, Pete sensed that the Lord was leading him in that direction, and he accepted the position.

He made the adjustment from military to civilian life quite easily. Pete really enjoyed his job. He had many responsibilities, one of which was setting up tours for individuals visiting the center. It gave him the opportunity to meet a lot of great people.

However, he found himself wavering once again on his conviction forbidding remarriage. Pete made the mistake of entertaining the possibility that it could perhaps be acceptable. Many well-meaning Christians were providing convincing arguments to that end, planting seeds of doubt in his mind. When he asked his family, he only became more confused. Some, like his mother, thought he should remarry, while others were adamantly against it.

The following spring, before completing his second term with Navigators, Pete returned home to Minnesota for an extended period to see family and attend his youngest brother's wedding. There he was introduced to his brother's new sister-in-law. She was an attractive woman who had lost her husband in a car accident. The two became very close over the course of the next few weeks. In fact, they started to date and subsequently fell in love. Though having known this woman for only a short time, he wanted to marry her.

One of the family members who had long opposed Pete remarrying was his brother Nick. Upon hearing of Pete's plans and in an effort to dissuade him from them, Nick asked him to attend a Rebuilders meeting. Though due back in Colorado soon to complete his term, he agreed to do so. Pete sought Pastor Hartzell's views on divorcees remarrying. In a very tender manner, the pastor discouraged him from taking on another wife and recommended that he read *Our Most Important Messages Grow Out of Our Greatest Weaknesses*. It was the same publication he had perused four years earlier while stationed in Japan.

While he appreciated Pastor Hartzell's concern, he was

undeterred. Pete was going to marry this woman. Besides, he rationalized, God would forgive him and provide the grace needed to have a happy marriage.

On the plane back to Colorado, Pete was trying to determine where and how he was going to ask for her hand. A couple of weeks passed, and he ended up calling and inviting her to fly out to Colorado Springs for a week. He wanted her to meet his friends at Navigators and take in some of the beautiful landscape but made no mention of his intentions to propose. She thought it would be fun and agreed to do so.

Upon her arrival, Pete popped the question. With great excitement, she said yes. They set the wedding date for that summer. There were many plans to be made. Living in separate states didn't necessarily help. Nonetheless, his fiancée returned to Minnesota a happy woman.

From the outside, everything looked well poised. It wasn't. Pete had absolutely no peace over the decision. He couldn't sleep at night and was not functioning properly during the day. God was making it evident where He stood.

To make His position extra clear, God would introduce into Pete's life people who, through their strong testimony on marriage, would convict his heart and turn him from such folly. One such individual was a pastor who had recently attended a conference at the center.

The seminar was on rebuilding broken marriages and the Lord's stance on divorce and remarriage. The pastor became convicted, as he had married numerous divorcees even though he knew it was wrong. That was going to change, however. Not only was he going to discontinue performing such ceremonies, he shared with Pete that he was going to rededicate himself to rebuilding the torn marriages amongst his parishioners. He asked Pete if he had read *Our Most Important Messages Grow Out of Our Greatest Weaknesses.* Looking grim, he acknowledged that he had. As the pastor continued to talk, all Pete could think about was removing himself from this man's presence. It wasn't a message he cared to hear.

Pete stayed the course. He was determined to follow through with his plans. God responded accordingly and turned up the heat a notch. He brought into Pete's life a woman who had just taken a tour of the center. She had learned that he, too, was originally from Minnesota and approached him to talk.

Having also heard he was divorced but engaged to be married, she felt compelled to share her testimony. On the brink of suicide, God had spared her, leading her to the Savior. Not long after, however, her husband left her for another woman and took the kids with him. Everyone told her to divorce him and find someone else. Nonetheless, she resisted. She had learned, through a workshop, God's ideal for marriage. The Lord called her to seek reconciliation. Though her husband was nowhere to be found, she was confident God would rebuild the marriage. She remained steadfast, and sure enough, four long years later, he returned home. He accepted Christ as Savior, and their children followed suit. Today, they have a beautiful relationship.

Pete acknowledged that it was a wonderful story. He reassured her, however, that God was leading him to remarry. Whether it was a blatant lie or an attempt to justify his intentions, Pete knew the truth deep down. He just wasn't willing to accept it.

Nonetheless, the woman found his response unsatisfactory and insisted that he come over to her house. She lived but a short distance from the center. She had something to give him. He reluctantly obliged. As they sat down to talk, she pleaded with him to reconsider. He was making a huge mistake. She had a small book for him to read entitled—you guessed it—*Our Most Important Messages Grow Out of Our Greatest Weaknesses*. Trying to be respectful, Pete said he would look it over and consider what she had shared.

As he departed, all Pete could do was shake his head in amazement. He was about to explode from the intense pressure God was applying. There was no refuge from it, and he was miserable. We worship a persistent God and thankfully so.

Having gate duty the following Saturday, Pete was responsible for screening guests and assisting them in finding their destinations. As is typical, the shift had a lot of down time. Consequently, Pete was taking the opportunity to reread the pamphlet. As he pondered what was written, he felt compelled to make a deal with God: If He would bring its author through the gate, Pete would call the wedding off. In other words, he would put God to the test.

Not an hour later, a car pulled up. Pete went through his normal routine. The gentleman, whom Pete did not recognize, gave his name and reason for visit. As he was preparing the guest pass, he thought the name looked familiar. And then it dawned on him. God had called his bluff. The pamphlet's author, Bill Gothard, was not five feet away, waiting for his badge. Unbelievable!!!

Finally convinced that God knew what was best for him, Pete forfeited control and became obedient. That night, he called his fiancée and shared that he would be unable to marry her. After he sought her forgiveness, he proceeded to explain why. She was understandably upset and hung up on him. Though ending the engagement was the right thing to do, he felt extremely bad for hurting this woman. Sin is not free. As Pete could attest, it has a cost. Later, however, he was delighted to hear that God had put into her life a good man.

With his commitment to Navigators over, Pete returned to Minnesota to assist with an ailing mother. This gave him the chance to share with her what God had done in his life. By His grace, he was able to lead her to Christ.

He started to attend Rebuilders on a regular basis. He had an opportunity to learn a great deal from John and Mary

Hartzell. He found their ministry immensely uplifting; it reinforced for him the boundless hope that can be had in Christ.

Pete also had the good fortune of becoming better acquainted with Chuck Raichert. He had met him a couple years prior when he was home for his brother's wedding. The two men quickly became friends. In fact, they became almost inseparable.

Over the course of the next six years, the relationship blossomed and came to epitomize Proverbs 27:17: "Iron sharpens iron, so one man sharpens another." Their desire to edify each other spilled over to others around them. Their complimentary gifts made them an effective tag team as they mentored countless others.

In 1990, God placed on Pete's heart the desire to serve overseas. He had been apprised of the significant global need for missionaries through presentations by Action International, a Christian recruitment team. After heavy prayer and many tears, he decided to join staff and move to Manila, where he would witness to urban poor and street children.

Pete continues that work today. Though it is difficult and at times heartbreaking, he has never been more joyful. While he never had kids of his own, Pete is now the surrogate father to several hundred beautiful Philippine children. His obedience in a time of great weakness proved to be fruitful, as God has blessed him for it. He can truly attest that "his most important messages did indeed grow out of his greatest weaknesses."

And they will for you, too, if you allow them.

6

Running on Empty

Mike and Michelle were the quintessential American couple. They were attractive, bright, and gregarious. Both had been raised in Christian homes and had accepted Christ as Savior at an early age.

From the outside, their relationship appeared strong. They seemed to enjoy each other's company and were content with the life they were living. In reality, their marriage was about to implode. They had become quite adept, particularly Michelle, at playing the role of happy couple so as to not arouse suspicion. The smiles they pasted on their faces in public were simply a facade to mask the pain and despair deep within.

Over the four plus years they had been married, the wear and tear of trying to live the Christian life had caught up to Michelle. She had reached a breaking point and found herself no longer capable of manufacturing the love required to be a wife as well as a follower of Christ. She wanted not only a separation but also a divorce from both her husband and her Lord.

While Mike knew things had become stagnant in their relationship, he had no idea that she had become so disillusioned. He clearly did not pick up on the severity of the warning signs that had surfaced. As husbands often do, Mike swept the concerns under the rug, hoping that they would just go away. They didn't. Consequently, he found himself at the eleventh hour in dire need of assistance. He was about to lose his wife.

Seeking intervention, Mike had heard of Chuck through his mother-in-law. She had attended Rebuilders several years earlier and knew the ministry well. She recommended that the couple start seeing him immediately. The question was whether Michelle would agree to meet.

Surprisingly, she did, albeit with reluctance. The three of them sat down in Chuck's office. Blunt and caustic with her comments, she made it clear she was done with Christianity. She was tired of playing church and the role of dutiful wife. It wasn't real anyhow, Michelle argued; the joy that believers around her were trumpeting was just a farce. She knew the Lord, but where was her peace?

Clearly, she was burned out. As Chuck explained, she was trying to live the Christian life on her own power, not Christ's. Because Michelle had cut herself off from the very lifeline that produces the energy to live abundantly, she had no way to recharge her battery when it became low. As a result, she became exhausted.

Unimpressed and defensive at this point, she countered that it was all a lie. No amount of theology was going to convince her that the despair she felt was somehow self-generated. God had let her down—not she, God. She had worked hard at doing the things Christians were supposed to do and yet she had no peace. Besides, she was at a place in her life where she simply needed to find herself—a euphemism for "I'm going to live my life the way I want to and no one is going to tell me otherwise."

Works don't produce fruit; they only produce fatigue, Chuck advised. Faith, which is a gift from God, bears fruit. We are simply the vessel, not the creator. Michelle had it completely backwards. In and of herself, she could achieve no good, only the outward appearance thereof. Consequently, her attempts to perform and impress had the exact opposite effect. Michelle found only weariness from such activities, not joy.

Mike was silent for most of the conversation. He did interject a few times, attempting to reassure Michelle of his love for her. Outside of that, he said nothing. Unmoved by her husband's sentiment or Chuck's admonishment, she remained steadfast in wanting out. Feeling that the conversation was going nowhere and angry with Chuck for asserting that she somehow played a role in her own misery, Michelle stormed out and drove away.

Mike just sat there in complete shock. He appeared completely confused as to where he was. Looking aimlessly around the room and with somber resignation, he concluded the marriage was over. Not knowing what else to do, he asked Chuck if the two of them could continue meeting. If he was going to make it through this trying time, he would need biblical direction.

They would meet weekly and talk on the phone several times between sessions. Chuck's task was to help Mike keep his eye on Christ; not only was his marriage in jeopardy, but his walk with Christ as well. He needed to learn patience and place his focus on strengthening his relationship with the Lord. God, in His own time, would work on Michelle's heart.

Unbeknownst to Chuck, Mike became impatient and went to Michelle's apartment to speak with her, even though she had a restraining order on him. He was going to take matters into his own hands. Upon arriving, he rang the buzzer to see if she would let him in. Recognizing his voice immediately, Michelle told him over the intercom to leave. He didn't and pushed the buzzer again. She threatened to call the police. Undeterred, he persisted. Realizing she wasn't going to budge, he eventually gave up and began walking towards his car. As he reached the sidewalk, Mike was greeted by two police officers. They handcuffed him, stuffed him into the backseat of the squad car, and escorted him to jail.

Once downtown, he was granted one phone call. It went to Chuck. Mike explained what had happened, and in no uncertain terms, let him know what he thought of his wife at that particular moment. Chuck's response was that what he did was wrong. Harassing his wife wasn't going to bring her back. He reinforced that it would be in God's timing, not his own. Mike needed to call her and seek forgiveness. Chuck instructed him to see if the police would allow another phone call given the first was made to his pastor. With a disgruntled voice, he reluctantly agreed. They granted his request, and he called her. Upon hearing his apology, Michelle made a sarcastic remark and abruptly hung up. And Mike spent the night in jail.

Having had considerable time to mull over the evening's events, Mike was about to explode when they released him the following morning. His first stop was to Chuck's office. Before Chuck could even greet him, Mike began blurting out justifications for his anger by listing all the invectives his wife had hurled at him. Chuck stopped him and made it very clear that God was in control. He needed to be patient. The Lord is bigger than our hearts and greater than our circumstances.

Though they would meet a couple more times, Mike broke off communication with Chuck shortly after his stint in jail. He wasn't showing up for meetings or calling. Week after week passed without word from him. Chuck feared that Mike had become unfaithful to his estranged wife and probably felt too guilty to face him.

A month after they had last talked, Mike finally showed up at Chuck's office. He looked as if he had been flattened by a bulldozer. Chuck's assumption about Mike's infidelity was unfortunately correct. After Michelle's rejection on the phone the night of his arrest, Mike explained, he relinquished any hope of ever getting her back. He basically gave up. Feeling lonely and indulged in self-pity, he decided to numb the pain by pursuing physical intimacy with a woman at work. However, realizing that this was bringing only greater despair, he ended the affair just prior to reconnecting with Chuck.

Mike was finally ready to heed Chuck's advice. He pored over Scripture and was encouraged by the promises outlined in it. Chuck advised him to love his wife regardless of her reaction. And Mike did just that. He gave her the space she requested, but when the opportunity arose, showered her with unconditional love.

To complicate matters, Mike learned that Michelle was pregnant, and it was unclear who the father was. Like Mike, she also had had an affair. The two men studied Galatians 6:1-2:

> Brethren, even if a man is caught in any trespass, you who are spiritual, restore such a one in a spirit of gentleness; looking to yourselves, lest you too be tempted. Bear one another's burdens, and thus fulfill the law of Christ.

Rather than get upset, as he would have in the past, Mike stayed the course. For the next few months, he and Chuck continued to meet. Though Michelle was still absent from the scene, Mike reported that the communications they were having were cordial and becoming increasingly productive. Both men were encouraged.

To Chuck's great delight, he received a call from Michelle soon thereafter. She wanted to know if he knew of anyone who would be willing to meet with her for counseling. She made it clear, however, that it was not to be him. Glad to facilitate, Chuck contacted an older couple he knew well in the church. They were excited to meet and looked forward to assisting in any way possible. Unfortunately, Michelle didn't show for the first meeting. Confused and somewhat frustrated, Chuck prayed that she would call again.

And a few days later, she did. She now wondered if he would be willing to meet with both her and Mike. Chuck was elated. After getting off the phone, he praised God. Perhaps she was ready to address the problems undermining her happiness.

She was now far along in her pregnancy. Though still depressed and feeling somewhat helpless, her heart was more receptive than it had been in the past. The change was due in large part to a praying husband who started to provide selfless and genuine care. He showed her the Christ she had long seen glorified through others, and it caught her attention.

Chuck opened with what he had told her months before: you cannot live the Christian life apart from Christ. He is your power and energy. He shared the following story.

> There was a woman who, while driving her car, ran out of gas. Needing to get the vehicle to a gas pump, she began pushing it. A stranger driving by saw her and stopped to ask if he could be of assistance. Between the two of them, they managed to get the car to a local filling station. Having no money, the woman asked to borrow some from the stranger. He gladly accommodated. Upon filling the tank, the woman thanked him for helping. As the man drove

away, he looked out his rearview mirror and to his astonishment found the woman still pushing the car.[9]

Why would someone in her position continue to push the car as if the tank were empty? Why do Christians rely upon their own finite resources when they have an infinite resource in Christ? Christ pays our debt by providing the money to purchase the gas, and the Holy Spirit furnishes the spark to ignite the fuel. But instead of getting into the car and turning the ignition, we continue to push until the point of exhaustion.

Mike, Michelle, and Chuck read, pondered, and then wholeheartedly prayed over Romans 8:31-39:

> What then shall we say to these things? If God is for us, who is against us? He who did not spare His own Son, but delivered Him up for us all, how will He not also with Him freely give us all things? Who will bring a charge against God's elect? God is the one who justifies; who is the one who condemns? Christ Jesus is He who died, yes, rather who was raised, who is at the right hand of God, who also intercedes for us. Who shall separate us from the love of Christ? Shall tribulation, or distress, or persecution, or famine, or nakedness, or peril, or sword? Just as it is written, 'FOR THY SAKE WE ARE BEING PUT TO DEATH ALL DAY LONG; WE WERE CONSIDERED AS SHEEP TO BE SLAUGHTERED.' But in all these things we overwhelmingly conquer through Him who loved us. For I am convinced that neither death, nor life, nor angels, nor principalities, nor things present, nor things to come, nor powers, nor height, nor depth, nor any other created thing, shall be able to separate us from the love of God, which is in Christ Jesus our Lord.

It was a defining moment for her. She was beginning to grasp the depth and unconditional nature of God's love. She no longer had to perform. Within days, Michelle rededicated her life to Christ. She realized that true peace could only be known when we forfeit control to God and allow Him to propel us forward. As Michelle learned the hard way, it is impossible to carve a joyful path apart from Christ. Prosperity can only be found in Him.

They started to attend Rebuilders and began working on restoring their relationship. The first step was to seek each other's forgiveness for the multiple offenses they had committed. They studied Colossians 3:12-13:

> And so, as those who have been chosen of God, holy and beloved, put on a heart of compassion, kindness, humility, gentleness and patience; bearing with one another, and forgiving each other, whoever has a complaint against any one; just as the Lord forgave you, so also should you.

While it is never easy or quick to undo pain and hurt, they placed their past in Christ's hands. It freed them to focus on the future.

Roughly a month later, Michelle gave birth to a beautiful boy. Chuck went to the hospital to visit, pray over the couple, and dedicate the child. It was joyous moment.

A few days later, Chuck received a surprising phone call from Mike. An attorney had advised him to have a blood test to see whether the baby was his. Finding this a bit disconcerting, Chuck asked bluntly, "Is Michelle your wife?" Mike indicated, "Yes." "Then that is your child," Chuck said without reservation. Realizing the attorney's counsel was foolish, Mike agreed and made a vow never to entertain the thought again. Today, they are doing well and are the proud parents of three beautiful children.

Christianity is not a question of role-play. You do not audition, nor are there any performance requirements. Your salvation and sanctification, quite simply, have nothing to do with you. They have everything to do with God. Both are gifts, not some recognition from God of human enterprise. It's important to understand the difference. A divine gift is the free expression of a God who neither needs nor requires anything from us to rule; on the other hand, the notion of divine reward reflects an erroneous attempt by man to earn favor from a God who is thought to be dependent upon those He created to carry out His will. It's as if, because of our works, God were now somehow in our debt and therefore required to repay us with salvation. God owes us nothing. We are a thimble of water in an ocean of righteousness.

What is so fascinating, however, is that while God doesn't need us, He does want us. He yearns to commune with His creation. It cost Him His Son to do so, but He calculated it was well worth the price. Wow! The God of the vast universe sacrificed His own so that He might forge a relationship with you and me. What a sobering thought!

As Chuck had explained to Michelle, while man is capable of manufacturing works, he is unable to produce fruit apart from faith. Good deeds alone are simply empty, energy-depleting exercises. They will cause you to run yourself right into the ground. When we exalt Christ and allow Him to lead, on the other hand, we produce a "fruit" that edifies and strengthens. "I can do all things through Him who strengthens me" (Philippians 4:13).

If we seek our strength through Christ, God will grant us an abundant life. This gift did not come cheaply; it required of Him more than we will ever comprehend. Please don't waste it.

7

Obediently Joyful

Carol led a beautiful life. She had five adoring children and an industrious husband who provided. Rick's strong work ethic enabled her to do what she enjoyed most—care for the family. Although he worked long hours trying to build a business from scratch, the family still managed to spend quality time together. Carol had it all.

The journey started in 1954 when they were college students. She was attending the University of Minnesota in Minneapolis and he Macalester College in St. Paul. Rick was tall, handsome, and polite. She felt like the center of the universe when they were together, for he hung on her every word. Carol had found the man of her dreams.

They married the following year. Over the course of the next twenty-one, they would bring into the world two wonderful boys and three lovely girls. They were certainly cruising on the highway of life; everything appeared to be well poised.

However, it all came to a crashing halt one dreary winter day in 1978. Rick announced that he wanted a divorce. He wasn't fulfilled in the relationship and had, in fact, been unfaithful to Carol. She was stunned. How could this be? They had such a solid marriage. How could things go from so good to so bad so quickly? While Carol knew she could be somewhat naive at times, Rick completely blind-sided her with this one. Apparently, he had been cheating on his wife for quite some time.

Though dejected and hurt, she knew that if Christ led the way, they could work through the agony and become whole again. Rick was not nearly as optimistic. He saw no hope and moved out.

Throughout their separation, Carol remained resolute and clung to her belief that the marriage was salvageable. Reconciliation was still possible. However, a rather harsh comment from Rick—"You'd better hire a good lawyer because I have hired the best"—finally convinced her that the union was over. The conclusion was extremely tough for her to reach.

She chose not to heed the threat. If divorce was the inevitable outcome, Carol did not want a nasty fight in court. Besides, she truly believed that Rick would treat her and the kids fairly.

Once again, however, Rick betrayed her trust. He was anything but equitable. When the divorce proceedings concluded, Rick, who was making a very handsome six-figure salary, was required to pay only a token of what Carol truly needed to properly raise the children. His obligation amounted to $750 a month in alimony the first five years and $100 a month per minor dependent in child support. Clearly, this was not going to make ends meet.

With five kids ranging in age from six to nineteen and no post-secondary degree, she needed help. While she had always relied on her strong faith, Carol would need to be completely grounded in Christ to make it through the challenges ahead.

To help her maintain focus, God placed in this woman's life other divorcees from within her congregation. They became a great source of encouragement and care. In addition, weekly gatherings provided much-needed companionship.

Though its purpose wasn't to commiserate, the group found itself increasingly frustrated with the larger church body. There was no formal ministry in place for those who, by no fault of their own, found themselves divorced. Individuals in the process of rebuilding their lives needed a structure. The void left them feeling ostracized and, to a certain extent, devalued.

They didn't just talk about it; they decided to act. They presented a proposal to John and Mary Hartzell. The couple was well known for reaching out to those who suffered from torn relationships. John thought the ministry was a wonderful idea and ran it past the church pastor. Agreeing that it could be of great benefit, he too wholeheartedly gave his endorsement. The year was 1980, and Rebuilder Ministries had just been born.

With the assistance of her friends at Rebuilders, Carol became a testimony to joyful obedience. Rather than cast God aside and seek her own solutions, she remained steadfast in the Word. She trusted that He would give her the strength and courage to weather the storms. One of her flagship verses was Isaiah 41:13: "For I am the Lord your God, who upholds your right hand, who says to you, 'Do not fear, I will help you.'" And He did.

While there were periods, especially early on, when the family lived from paycheck to paycheck, Carol was never without steady employment. While her positions were never glamorous (teller, receptionist, personal administrator, and sales associate), they did allow her to raise the family in a dignified fashion.

One specific manifestation of God's steady presence in

Carol's life was her compassion. Instead of becoming absorbed in self-pity, she reached out. In fact, for the first three Christmases after the divorce, she spent the day assisting the homeless at a local soup kitchen. Her children were with their father, and, rather than stay home and feel sorry for herself, Carol chose to help those who were in greater need than she.

Take a moment and think about this. Christ took a woman who had been dumped and left with five kids to support and gave her the grace to place the troubles of others above her own. Clearly, the Holy Spirit was alive and well in Carol's heart.

> But the fruit of the Spirit is love, joy, peace, patience, kindness, goodness, faithfulness, gentleness, self-control; against such things there is no law. Now those who belong to Christ Jesus have crucified the flesh with its passions and desires (Galatians 5:22-24).

She would spend the next two decades subscribing to a literal interpretation of Philippians 4:4: "Rejoice in the Lord always; again I will say, rejoice!" Notice that the verse doesn't read, "Rejoice in the Lord when times are good or you feel up to it." We are to rejoice in the Lord *always*. And that is exactly what Carol did. She delighted in God, enabling herself to meet the demands of being a single parent.

In 1998, Carol found herself without a job. Her employer of the previous thirteen years had gone out of business. Though no longer supporting a large family, she couldn't afford to retire. Carol wasn't old enough to qualify for Social Security or Medicare. She began babysitting four days a week for one of her sons and also took on evening and weekend work at a department store. While this was not an ideal situation, she had little choice.

It wouldn't be long, however, before her formal working days would come to end.

In March of 2001, all five of Carol's children had gathered at the house for a send-off party. Her daughter who lived on the West Coast was departing soon, and the siblings wanted to say good-bye. It had been a long time since just the six of them were alone together. While she loved her sons- and daughters-in-law very much, it was special to have just her kids there. They had been through so much together. And the fact that they were still good friends and enjoyed being together meant a great deal to her. Unbeknownst to Carol, there was another reason behind their gathering.

After everyone had finished eating, her oldest child, Matt, stood up from the dinner table and announced that there was some business that needed attention. Confused and a bit curious, Carol sat back and listened intently. The five children and their spouses, he explained to his mother, had gotten together the previous week to take the families swimming at a local pool. At one point, they began to reminisce about various childhood experiences and the great many sacrifices their mother had made. It was now time, the ten agreed, to give something back. With complete unanimity, they decided to provide her the financial means to retire.

"How can you do this? You all have your own families to support," Carol quickly responded. Matt pointed out that God had richly blessed each of them and that they could now in turn bless her. Overwhelmed with emotion, she struggled to find the words to adequately express her love and appreciation. She still fights back the tears today when telling this wonderful story.

I asked Carol what her biggest regret was with regard to the divorce. I was sure that she would comment about the long hours at work or the extreme loneliness, but she didn't. She focused on the children. They had been cheated. While they were all involved in many activities growing up, more times than not they performed them without the proud gaze of a parent in the audience. It hurt her dearly that she was unable to attend more frequently.

Being the joyful, upbeat person she is, Carol closed our talk with a word of encouragement. "God is truly all we have. He is the only One we can completely depend upon. While man, with his fallen nature, will surely disappoint, God never will." In an act of faith, she reached out her hand in 1979, and God took it; He has gently led the way ever since. And while there have been many bumps on the road, it has been a glorious ride, she assured me.

Upon completing this chapter's rough draft, I sent a copy to Carol for her editorial review. After she returned it, I found what she had written at the bottom of the last page too wonderful to omit.

> Time does not heal all things, but it does reveal God's work in our lives. He has revealed to me that He can be trusted, He always honors His word, He hears our cries and meets our every need. He is holy, and He is sufficient. I've learned I can trust Him for what I do know but also for all the things I do not know. It's His character that comforts me daily.
>
> Rejection was a painful experience, and I struggled with it for a long time until I realized that in reality only Rick had rejected me, not my friends, family, or children, and certainly not God. Every tear I shed He was longing to wipe away.
>
> Rick married shortly after our divorce was final, but that relationship only lasted a year. He is currently married to his fourth wife, and we are all hoping he makes a good success of this one. We all want him to be happy. God forgives and so must we.

Will you let God be a source of comfort and wipe away your tears? He is waiting with tissue in hand.

8

Delighting in Him

Jean met Rod on a blind date in 1964. She was attracted to him for many reasons, but one in particular. He was something her father hadn't been during her youth: sober. While never emotionally or physically abusive, Jean's dad was indeed a drunk. Excessive drinking hurts all families, and Jean's was no exception. It was especially difficult on her mother. Jean made a vow as a young woman to never marry a man who drank. She didn't want to relive the nightmare.

The relationship with Rod was going well. It seemed to be a perfect fit. The first real test came in 1966 when Rod was drafted into the service and moved from Minnesota to Clinton-Sherman Air Force Base in Oklahoma.

The distance confirmed for Jean that this was the man for her. Far from diminishing, her feelings for him only grew over the many months they were apart. Upon returning home on leave almost three years after they had begun dating, he proposed. Jean enthusiastically accepted. Rod would provide the exit she had long sought. She being Lutheran and he Catholic, a traditional wedding wasn't going to work; they decided to elope. Jean prepared herself for a nice, quiet life in Oklahoma, hundreds of miles away from the chaos she endured for so long.

Not three days into the marriage, she learned that the man she loved had developed a taste for liquor while in the service. While Rod was, at least initially, merely a social drinker, Jean couldn't help but replay over and over again her past, wondering whether history was about to repeat itself. The irony was almost too much. Jean feared that she had entered into the very situation she thought she was escaping. In disbelief, she called her mother in Minnesota, hoping to come home. Jean's mom gave her some very sound advice: she must remain with her husband and learn to love him like God does.

As difficult as the situation was, she stuck it out because of her care and concern for Rod. During their first two years of marriage, they saw little of each other since he was often stationed overseas. She did manage, however, to get pregnant during one of his leaves. She would deliver a son to a man she barely knew and didn't completely trust. It was as if they were complete strangers.

Rod left the service in 1970 and moved the family to Minnesota. He found a job working for an insulation company that he ended up purchasing a few years later. Though Rod continued to drink, he was able to function, relatively speaking, quite well and ran a successful business. As he was home every night, the long periods of separation were now in the past.

Unfortunately, while closer in physical proximity, the two were still worlds apart emotionally. Neither Rod nor Jean knew Christ. Consequently, they had no means through which to understand their situation and the sin that had created it. Oh, they played the church game but had no real interest in Jesus. Despite the erected walls, they added to their family a second son. As is the case in many strained marriages, the husband focused on work and the wife on the kids. While there were good times, the disconnect was clearly evident, and it was widening.

Rod, over the course of the marriage, failed time and time again to comprehend and appreciate his wife's increased sensitivity to the drinking and the issues it created. At the same time, Jean failed to understand the immense pressure she had placed on her husband to meet what most would consider unattainable expectations. One misunderstanding simply fed the other, creating a vicious cycle that came to a head in a somewhat predictable fashion almost twenty years into the marriage. It was 1985. Rod had found another woman. Naturally, Jean was extremely hurt, although not entirely surprised. They had, after all, been moving in two separate directions.

Nonetheless, she was resolute in attempting to mend the relationship. She asked him to try counseling. While he initially agreed, Rod eventually concluded that there was no turning back. He couldn't reverse what he had started with this other woman and soon moved out.

Thankfully, a neighbor who knew the Lord befriended Jean and invited her to attend BSF (Bible Study Fellowship). Though somewhat intimidated, Jean did approach the leader of the study group for guidance. Jean shared with her the problems in the marriage and explained how she blamed herself. If only she were prettier, more caring, or less demanding; if only God would bring Rod back; if only she could have another shot at pleasing him.

Realizing that Jean needed more intensive assistance than she could provide, the woman referred her to Rebuilder Ministries. She had heard that Pastors Hartzell and Raichert were doing great things—perhaps they could be of some guidance.

At Rebuilders, Jean was exposed to true biblical principle. She realized that her focus was misplaced. While she had been hoping that God might change the circumstances or Rod, she in fact needed Him to change *her*, and not merely in outward appearance. Jean's demanding character was not the core problem, only a symptom. The true ailment was her not knowing Christ. She needed a new heart—one that He alone controlled. Realizing this, Jean relinquished the reins and accepted Christ as Savior.

God taught her amazing lessons that summer. There wasn't a thing she could do for Rod; she needed to release him to the Lord. Her task was to improve her own walk. Through the support of John and Mary Hartzell, Jean was able to endure the hardships one day at a time. Psalm 139:14 became a staple in her life: "I will give thanks to Thee, for I am fearfully and wonderfully made; wonderful are Thy works, and my soul knows it very well."

Over the course of the next year or so, Rod threatened several times to serve divorce papers. Still, Jean made it clear that she wouldn't sign them. As Rebuilders taught, divorce is not part of God's design. Her unsaved family, however, was telling her something very different: she needed to take the initiative and dissolve the marriage. She deserved to find someone who would love her, they argued. Thankfully, she didn't listen to them. Rod was her husband; she would not divorce him.

Then, completely out of character, Jean dropped her guard. She entered into a relationship with another man. She knew from the very beginning that it was wrong and, during the course of the affair, wept herself to sleep every night. Feeling too guilty to face anyone, she stopped attending Rebuilders, the ministry that she had wrapped her life around the past year. She cut herself off from the very people that she had grown to love.

What happened? She had been steadfast in her desire to please God but then, all of a sudden, took a detour. Jean attributed it primarily to a failure to be in the Word. Rather than draw her energy from Christ directly, she relied solely on the accounts of others. Without God's inspiration through Scripture, she was without a shield and susceptible to attack. The hedonism of the world began seeping into her thinking. Without biblical defense, she listened and acted upon her impulses.

Knowing her sin hurt God and feeling extremely isolated, Jean turned from it and ended the relationship. She brought her two-month hiatus from Rebuilders to an end and took her burdens to John and Mary Hartzell, asking that they forgive her. Graciously, they did, but made it clear that she would also need to seek forgiveness from her husband. As difficult as it was to hear, Jean agreed to do so. In preparation for the encounter, Pastor John walked her through Hebrews 12:1-2:

> Therefore, since we have so great a cloud of witnesses surrounding us, let us also lay aside every encumbrance, and the sin which so easily entangles us, and let us run with endurance the race that is set before us, fixing our eyes on Jesus, the author and perfecter of faith, who for the joy set before Him endured the cross, despising the shame, and has sat down at the right hand of the throne of God.

When she asked for Rod's forgiveness, he didn't quite know what to say. He was shocked and couldn't believe Jean was capable of infidelity. Rod did forgive her but clarified that his desire to proceed with the divorce had not changed.

It wasn't until 1989, however, after three years of separation, that he took serious action to end their marriage. Knowing she wouldn't agree to the divorce, he had papers drafted from "default court," as Jean called it. When one party thinks the marriage is still reconcilable but the other doesn't, the latter can pursue a default dissolution. In effect, it ends the legal recognition of the marriage with the consent of only one spouse.

Rod informed Jean of his intentions, indicating that the hearing would be held relatively soon and that her presence was not required. Knowing it would not be easy for Rod, she asked if she could be there to help him through it. He was dumbfounded but granted her request.

The day of the hearing arrived. Jean was accompanied by a close friend. On the way to the courthouse, Jean asked if she could pull her car over and pray. They both sought God's face, asking that hearts change and that the Savior shine.

When Rod introduced Jean to his attorney, she looked puzzled and asked Jean to explain. She loved her husband and was there to support him, Jean responded. The attorney was confused but touched, and the two women embraced.

While awaiting their turn, they sat and listened to the cases that proceeded theirs, noting the procedure. It stipulated that the attorney ask the client whether he or she felt the marriage was irreconcilable. If the client answered yes, the judge would then proceed to the conditions of the divorce. Overhearing this, Rod turned to his attorney and directed her to not ask him that question when their turn came. Something about it had stirred his soul. Clearly, God was beginning to convict him.

When their number was called, Rod surprised everyone by asking Jean to approach the bench with him and his attorney. As the three drew near, the judge looked strangely at Rod and asked who the additional person was. He answered. The judge explained to Jean that her consent wasn't required to end the marriage. If she wanted to stop the proceedings and seek legal counsel, however, she had every right to do so. She responded that she was aware of all of this and went on to clarify her rationale for attending. Somewhat stunned, the judge began to examine the documents. Unlike the other cases he had just presided over, he took his time with theirs. He slowly perused the details surrounding Rod's request for divorce.

The judge would periodically raise his head and look inquisitively at either Jean or Rod. After a complete review of the case, he pointed his finger at Rod and sternly told him that he valued the institution of marriage and did not take divorce lightly. Thus, if he were to rule in Rod's favor, Rod would be required to fulfill to the letter the obligations outlined in the document—otherwise, he personally would have him brought back to court.

The judge then turned to Jean and explained that he would reluctantly grant the divorce. If she had any problems, Jean was to call him. After they were excused, Rod hurried out of the room. Jean followed quickly behind. In the hallway, he suddenly stopped, turned, and, after a moment of hesitation, hugged her, profusely apologizing for what she had just gone through.

Jean knew God was pricking at his heart. Nonetheless, three months later, Rod married the woman for whom he had left Jean. Until that point, she had still clung to the hope that reconciliation was possible. It was a sad day for her, but she knew she wasn't alone. Though she had lost her earthly husband, her Heavenly One would always be by her side, as would her friends at Rebuilders. Chuck and Polly Raichert helped immensely during this difficult time. They assisted Jean as she kept her eyes on Christ.

Rod's second marriage would last roughly five years. His new wife came to know the Lord during the time they were married and became convicted of her role in Rod's divorce—so much so that she actually sought Jean's forgiveness. She confessed that during the many years Jean and Rod were separated, she had stymied several of his attempts to return to his family.

Though Rod had stopped drinking and was becoming more responsible, his current wife still felt compelled to leave him. Jean advised against it. Two wrongs don't make a right, she explained. Nonetheless, they divorced.

Rod and Jean started talking more frequently after this. His heart was becoming more and more tender. An associate at work had introduced him to a group of pastors who, like Rod, enjoyed golf. Their conversations went well beyond just the sport, however. The men witnessed to Rod and tried to show him his need for Christ.

He listened but made no decisions. Still unrepentant and blind to his follies, Rod ignored the advice of many and eventually married again. His third wife had also just recently divorced. Predictably, the union lasted a very short time—less than two years.

Married three times and divorced three times, Rod sought in marriage what could only be found in Christ—acceptance and unconditional love. He finally came to that realization—in part because of what he continued to see in Jean. She had gone through tremendous heartache yet maintained a delightful and joyful heart; this captured his attention and made him curious. He wanted the very same thing. Desiring to see God work in his own life, Rod repented of his sin and accepted Jesus Christ as Savior.

Through Christ, Rod proved to be dependable and trustworthy. Today, he financially supports all three former wives and has a cordial, nurturing relationship with each, particularly Jean. The two talk several times a week. Rod also rebuilt his relationship with his two sons. They had been hurt by the tumult of the separation and subsequent divorces. Rod took responsibility and sought their forgiveness. He is now an integral part of their lives.

In talking about what God had done for her many years ago and for Rod more recently, Jean still stands in awe of His incredible power to change hardened hearts. "Now to Him who is able to do exceeding abundantly beyond all that we ask or think, according to the power that works within us" (Ephesians 3:20). As Jean passionately explains, God has been and continues to be exceedingly abundant with His blessing.

She continues to wear her wedding ring—the only one she has ever worn—to this day.

9

To the Ends of the Earth and Back

Thirty years old and full of life, Bob enthusiastically predicted that 2001 would be a great year. He and his wife, Kristi, were extremely excited about the prospect of becoming missionaries to Mexico. They had successfully cleared all the major preparatory hurdles except for securing financial support.

That May, in the midst of building their contributor base, Kristi received an alarming phone call from a friend living in Louisiana. Jenny, who had moved to New Orleans some twelve months earlier, was frantic and almost unintelligible. After calming down somewhat, she managed to convey, between intermittent sobs, the reason for her call. She had fallen away from the Lord and into the arms of a Lebanese man whose character she was beginning to doubt.

Kazim, Jenny proceeded to explain, seemed very nice when they first met. She enjoyed his company a great deal, as well as that of his Middle Eastern friends. Over the course of the past few months, however, the relationship had begun to change. He was becoming more and more cunning and self-contradictory. Little by little, things were no longer adding up, and it was making her nervous.

What created the hysteria, thus prompting the phone call, though, were Kazim's recent attempts to convince her to move to Egypt with him. He had become increasingly insistent. As Jenny provided a more detailed history of the relationship, Kristi became more and more concerned.

Sensing a trap, she advised her friend to remove herself from the situation as soon as possible. In fact, Kristi proposed, Jenny should consider returning to Minnesota to live with her and Bob until things settled down. Having no other option, Jenny accepted the invitation and made the move.

It would not be long, however, before her urge to rejoin Kazim emerged. Kristi reminded her friend of the dangers this group presented. They were bad news, and she needed to completely divorce herself from them. Jenny took heed. She made a commitment to try to suppress the desire.

A small problem remained. She had grabbed only a handful of items prior to leaving Kazim and needed the balance of her belongings. Reluctant to let Jenny return alone and risk being sucked back in, Kristi offered to drive her to Louisiana and help pack.

The 1,300-mile trip, considered nothing more than a minor inconvenience initially, would usher into Bob and Kristi's life twelve months of great trial. Kristi's efforts to secure a friend's safety would end up jeopardizing her own and in turn compromise not only the couple's missionary plans but also their marriage. It's a story almost too inconceivable to believe.

As the two headed for New Orleans, Kristi had no intention of interacting with the group. She wanted to collect Jenny's things and get out of there. When they arrived, it became apparent that she might not have a choice in the matter. Kazim, who lived in the same complex, was standing outside with several of his friends as they pulled up. It was as if they were expecting the women. Not wanting to solicit any attention, Kristi said little to anyone. She just focused on the task at hand and began loading the car.

Even though somewhat scared and in a hurry, Kristi let curiosity take over and began eavesdropping on the men. To her surprise, what she could make of their exchange was neither caustic nor derogatory; it was actually quite congenial. With her interest piqued, Kristi began listening even more intently. What she heard continued to dumbfound her. They weren't the barbarians and brainwashers she had been led to believe. Her concerns sufficiently alleviated, she took the bold move of engaging them in conversation.

After a pleasant exchange, Kristi returned to packing. To the women's dismay, they were not able to fit all of Jenny's belongings in the car. The two loaded what they could and headed north. The ride home, while long, afforded Kristi the opportunity to think over what had just transpired. She had left Minnesota with a certain preconceived notion about the group of men and returned home rather enlightened. Though certainly unusual, she found these individuals very interesting.

Kristi shared her discoveries with Bob. He paid little attention to her, though; the missionary trip was his sole focus. But she wasn't completely forthcoming, either. There was something she had left out that certainly would have generated a different response from her husband had it been disclosed. In the course of getting better acquainted with these men, she became particularly fond of one of them. Assad was very charming, and Kristi could sense, as they talked, that she was developing an emotional interest in him. In fact, the attraction was so strong that she initiated a secret correspondence shortly after her return to Minnesota.

In mid-June, the two women decided to make a second trek to gather the last remaining items in Jenny's apartment. Meanwhile, Bob continued to focus on Mexico. It wasn't until he received a phone call from Kristi while she was in New Orleans that he started to become concerned. She indicated that her trip home would be delayed due to weather and other unforeseeable circumstances. Under normal conditions, this wouldn't have raised any red flags. But given the nature of the trip and the fact that Kristi was uncharacteristically vague and evasive, Bob became suspicious. He knew his wife well, and something wasn't right. She was lying to him.

Confused and upset, Bob jumped on a flight to New Orleans to find the women and bring them home. (Kristi had given him the address before departing on her first trip.) Once there, he said little outside of instructing the two to pack quickly. As they walked towards the car to leave, Kristi shouted to Assad, who was standing on the balcony, that she loved him. Bob was standing but five feet from her when she did so. He was stunned! One moment they were preparing for missionary work, and the next it was as if he was pulling his wife from the arms of a stranger.

Needless to say, the trip home was long. Bob, Kristi, and Jenny traveled the first 200 miles in complete silence. Bob eventually pulled the car over so that he and his wife could go for a walk and talk in private. As they worked through the events of the previous few weeks, Kristi acknowledged that the relationship was inappropriate. Although she said little else, she promised to end it.

And rather than deal with the weighty issues confronting their marriage and aggressively address what led his wife to seek companionship in another man, Bob acted as if nothing had happened. In reality, he was shaken. His world had just been turned completely upside down. This man didn't know whether he was coming or going.

Not sure where to turn, he buried himself, once again, in trip preparation. This time was different, however. Though the intensity of the planning hadn't changed, the reason for it had. What had been conceived as a means to show Christ became a shelter from which to avoid Him.

Predictably, the marriage continued to spiral downward. Communication all but halted. They sought counseling, but the day before their second session, Kristi ended up pulling a fast one on Bob. He had dropped her off at a clinic where she was being treated for ongoing depression. Instead of going to the appointment, she called a cab and headed to the airport. Kristi returned to Assad in Louisiana.

Shocked into the realization that the illicit relationship was far from over, Bob and his father-in-law raced to New Orleans to try to get her back. Thankfully, she agreed to talk. The couple met in a restaurant parking lot. As Bob began expressing his anguish, he noticed that she wasn't wearing her wedding ring. Rather than risk igniting an argument over it, he said nothing, preferring to reach out and hold her hand in a gesture of love. Kristi withdrew.

Despite her cold disposition, Bob came close to persuading her to return. But as time went on, she became progressively concerned that they were perhaps being watched. Anxious and fearful, she suggested they wrap up before getting caught.

"Before getting caught? We are husband and wife for goodness sake," Bob thought to himself. Part of him felt compelled simply to grab Kristi, escort her to the car, and end the nonsense. This was ridiculous. But deep down he wanted to be chosen, not merely obeyed. Besides, if he forced her to come home, she would just turn around and fly back anyhow.

Hoping that Kristi's father could talk some sense into her, Bob fetched him from inside the restaurant. She ran to him as he walked out, and the two embraced. They had a heartfelt conversation. Unfortunately, even her dad couldn't convince her that she was in danger and needed to return with them.

Deflated, Bob gave his wife the night to think it over. The next morning the two men returned to Minnesota without her. She had chosen Assad and in so doing broke her husband's heart.

Bob had most likely just lost his beautiful wife and the mother of his three children. The trip home was but a blur both literally and figuratively. He drove exceedingly fast, twenty to thirty miles per hour over the speed limit, the entire way. It was as if he was trying to outrun his problems.

Over the course of the next few months, Kristi would return to Minnesota for several short stints, but just to grab a few things and then quickly leave again. Each time she showed up, Bob pleaded with her to stay. And with each departure, she took a piece of his hope with her. Never sure which "pop-in" would be the last, he knew eventually it was coming. (That day ended up being October 29th.)

As November came and went and the weeks grinded into months without word from her, Bob became extremely restless. By January 2002, he had had enough of waiting around and decided to make another attempt to get his wife back.

However, disheartening news greeted him as he landed in New Orleans. In December 2001, Kristi had moved with Assad to Bahrain, a series of islands off the coast of Saudi Arabia. This was not long after the terrorist attacks of September 11th, and hostility was high. In fact, the U.S. State Department had declared this particular country inhospitable to Americans and recommended no travel there. It was also known for its prostitution industry. Women from around the world were imported, in effect, and then sold into harlotry.

Unaware whether his wife was dead or alive, Bob needed help. He was driving himself crazy with worry, frustration, and anger. Realizing the burden was too great to bear alone, he sought help. He found it at Rebuilder Ministries.

Chuck, among others, taught Bob to let God be God—he needed to surrender his anxieties to the cross. He did so, and to the glory of God, found some relief. He relied upon a multitude of verses to sustain him, and one in particular. It was Philippians 4:6-7:

> Be anxious for nothing, but in everything by prayer and supplication with thanksgiving let your requests be made known to God. And the peace of God, which surpasses all comprehension, shall guard your hearts and your minds in Christ Jesus.

With the Savior guiding him, Bob was able to endure the pain and assemble some level of sanity.

Thankfully, in late January, after three long and excruciating months, he received an e-mail from Kristi. Glory to God! She was alive! While she wasn't allowed to tell him where she was (though he knew), parts of the letter hinted towards her wanting to come home. (Because the family sponsoring her in Bahrain was monitoring her communications, Kristi had to "code" the e-mails to avoid alerting suspicion.)

In e-mailing her back, Bob shared some disturbing news. Her father had recently been diagnosed with prostate cancer. Though the prognosis was good, Bob prayed that this development might help convince his wife to return. And God answered. Kristi, on her own, devised a plan to tell the host family that her dad was deathly ill, and that she needed to see him as soon as possible. Kristi and Bob would talk on the phone roughly six times during the next three months strategizing the return. (The family in Bahrain trusted her enough to go unsupervised for a large portion of the workday. This allowed her to secretly use a street pay phone to make the calls.)

Assad and the host family would grant her request only on the condition that she initiate divorce proceedings while home. Having convinced them that she would, Kristi was allowed in April to return to the U.S. As soon as she landed in Germany, her first layover, she called Bob to let him know that she had been released and would be in New York City the following day. Without telling her, Bob booked a flight to meet her there. He wanted to show Kristi how excited he was to have her back.

As he waited in the airport, his mind raced with various images of what she might look like having been gone for so long. Would she be battered and bruised? Would he even recognize her? As Kristi walked through the gates, Bob was astonished. She was as beautiful and healthy as ever. What a sight for sore eyes. He ran up and embraced her, almost reluctant to let go. It was April 27th—almost six months to the day after she had vanished.

The weeks that followed were difficult. Kristi carried a heavy burden. She was repeatedly tempted to run from all the pain her sin had caused. How could she possibly repair the damage, Kristi asked in agony? It seemed easier simply to slip away and let the family move on without her.

She was feeding herself lies. Yes, she had done some bad things. And yes, people got hurt because of them. What she failed to realize in her state of despair was that through Christ all things are possible, including reconciliation. It would not be easy. Seeking and obtaining bondage-breaking forgiveness never is. But it is always worth every bead of sweat and every teardrop.

They would seek help from several third parties, one of whom was Chuck. He knew the story well. Along with his congregation and those at Rebuilders, Chuck had been praying for Kristi's return the entire time she was overseas.

Chuck could empathize with the guilt Kristi was feeling. Beating herself up emotionally was not the answer, however.

Though she was right to take her sin seriously, he pointed out that her self-loathing was, in fact, unproductive. Kristi's focus on her own misery was only suffocating her and crowding out the very One who could remove the anguish.

Chuck reminded Kristi that Christ died for all sinners and to cleanse all sins. He read to her Colossians 2:13-14:

> And when you were dead in your transgressions and the uncircumcision of your flesh, He made you alive together with Him, having forgiven us all our transgressions, having cancelled out the certificate of debt consisting of decrees against us and which was hostile to us; and He has taken it out of the way, having nailed it to the cross.

Through the Savior, the blemishes of one's past could be removed. There was hope, but she needed to embrace it.

It's truly miraculous how God takes care of His wayward sheep. Rather than allow Kristi to continue down her path of self-destruction, He interceded in a most powerful manner. She was attending a Sunday morning service not long after talking to Chuck when the Lord revealed His grace. He made it clear that her despair was not part of His design. What better proof could there be than the cross? The stain-removing power of the Savior struck her during the sermon with such force that Kristi went forward for the altar call that followed. In tears and on her knees, she rededicated her life to Christ. It was the beginning of what has been a time of reconciliation and growth.

It was also the start of a rededication to her marriage. The key to the closeness she and her husband now enjoy has been staying connected emotionally and praying together over the Word of God. Let me rephrase: The key has been staying connected emotionally *by* praying together over the Word of God. The *and* implies that these two realities are merely parallel and independent of each other. This is not the case. One clearly causes the other.

In making this distinction, I was inspired by John Piper, who in his book *Desiring God*, points out that the chief end of man is not, as an old tradition suggests, "to glorify God *and* enjoy Him forever." It is, rather, "to glorify God *by* enjoying Him forever."[10] Though illustrating a different point, Piper beautifully hits upon a larger truth: God is the channel through which things happen. To believe in coincidence, luck, fate, star alignment, human effort, and so on, is to practice idolatry and to rob your God of His glory. All blessings, big and small, are solely and completely willed by Him. These include marital unity and prosperity.

I recognize that to the evangelical Christian this seems painfully self-evident. The fact is, however, that each and every one of us, with different frequencies and levels of absurdity, messes up this glorious truth. We have all tried to manufacture, to one extent or another, our own happiness. And we have all fallen flat on our faces because of it. Bob and Kristi were no exception.

They learned the hard way that when God's Word is not center stage, Satan will seize the opportunity and usher into the home vulnerability, temptation, and division. The great deceiver took God-honoring activities—missionary preparation and a woman's effort to ensure a friend's safety—and used them as leverage to attack the marriage. The only reason Satan enjoyed the success he did was that the couple's relationship, at the time of the assaults in early 2001, was not girded by Scripture. As Bob now freely admits, they had made fund raising a higher priority than couple devotions. Satan saw his lead and took advantage of it.

Those days are in the past. God is now piloting their marriage. Admittedly, the relationship has been under some strain recently. They not long ago gave birth to their fourth child, and for reasons not yet diagnosed, the infant rests in only twenty-minute intervals and needs to be held the balance. Though sleep-deprived and unable to spend as much time in the Word together as they might hope, the two know better than most that God is the glue that keeps marriages and all biblical relationships from splintering. As tired as they may be, their hope now resides in Him! And yours can too.

10

The Big Miracle in the Little Man

It was quickly shaping up to be the defining moment of Rob's young life. Though not exactly sure how or why it came to be, he found himself at lunch sitting with and talking to the most beautiful girl in the high school. The two had gone well beyond cafeteria pleasantries and were thoroughly enjoying each other's company. Rob had her in stitches.

As they continued a banter that bordered on flirtation, he was becoming increasingly confident that she was attracted to him. He might actually have a shot at a date with her. He was feeling seven feet tall. It was a moment of pure euphoria.

Then, as if to culminate some type of cruel hoax, the beauty queen nonchalantly and somewhat callously blurted out, "You know Rob, if only you were a foot taller, we could have so much fun together."

Rob recoiled. He would have preferred that the girl take the knife from her tray and stab him in the heart. The wound would have been far less painful and would have healed far more quickly than the emotional anguish she unknowingly caused. He was nothing but numb. Just when Rob thought he had a chance at finding a girlfriend, a very pretty one at that, the rug is pulled from underneath him, and he is sent reeling once again.

Those few words would have a reverberating effect on Rob for a long time to come. You see, Rob stands but 4' 10" tall and weighs eighty-five pounds soaking wet. He is, by conventional standards, a very tiny man.

The ailment that stunted his growth occurs in just one in a million people. His parents had always taught him, however, that God had made their son with unique design and special purpose. And for the majority of his childhood, he bought into the notion. Yes, he would take a few jabs here and there in elementary school. After a few tears and some reassuring words from his mother, however, he went back to believing that he was exceptionally blessed.

As he got older and the disparity in size between him and his peers grew, the cruel remarks became more scathing and frequent. It was only a matter of time before his confidence collided with the prejudices of his teenage nemeses.

Don't be misled. Rob was not naive; he knew full well that his height created barriers. But prior to the cafeteria debacle, he had still held out hope that some girl somewhere might look past his physical characteristics and see him for who he truly was: a fun, caring person.

As Rob stood there in shock and realized that this last glimmer of hope had just been extinguished, he was forced to confront a truth he had long feared and refused to accept: his stature didn't make him special—it made him a freak. It wasn't a gift from God but a curse.

The bouts of depression that had popped up in his youth became manic when he reached his teens. He had lost all hope of anyone ever becoming romantically interested in him. On top of this overwhelming gloom lay a thick, impenetrable coat of anger. Rob was mad at everything and everyone. He had, to say the least, a sour disposition. He was so crabby, in fact, that his parents nicknamed him "Oscar the Grouch." His resentment ran particularly deep towards his Maker. Why would God do this to him? Why would He humiliate him like this?

Rob's bitterness would simmer for a few more years. What he didn't realize at the time was that he never really knew God. Oh, he believed in the Bible and went to church every Sunday, but he had never repented of his sins and placed his full trust in the Savior. Because he didn't know Jesus and have a true relationship with Him, Rob was unable to correctly interpret the reasons behind the various conditions he faced.

His misunderstanding didn't deter God from intervening, however. As Rob's height and the hindrances it presented continued to gnaw at him, God was quietly working in the background. He was preparing him for what would be the first in a series of changes and refinements in his life—the first of which entailed securing a saving knowledge of Christ. It was none too soon; Rob was sinking and sinking fast.

God brought him to this crossroads in 1981, when Rob was twenty. He had a choice to make: either accept God's Word or reject it. He could not have it both ways. With a touch of His grace, Rob saw the waywardness of his thinking and began to embrace his Savior.

God reinforced the message later that summer at a Bible seminar. He impressed a couple of truths upon Rob. First, that the world consists of two schools of thought: God's way and man's. One cannot subscribe to both and prosper as a Christian. And second, that God is in control and does nothing without just purpose and cause. His actions are always for His glory and thus our good.

These truths had considerable poignancy for Rob. His

smallness was not the result of some flippant or careless whim on God's part. It was by design and for his benefit. As a result, the extensive anger that had been tainting Rob's view of God for the past couple of years lifted.

Rob's size was, in fact, a blessing. God made him small to protect him. Indeed, Rob held in the far recesses of his heart certain desires which, had they been tested, would have caused him to badly stumble. In addition, he most assuredly would not have met his wonderful future wife had he sported a "normal" build.

Rob married this caring person in 1983. Rebecca was the type of woman he had always longed for, and he was joyful. God blessed him with someone to love who would love him back. Happy ending to a wonderful story, right? Not quite.

By the late 80s and early 90s, the marriage had already endured significant blows. Rob had become cold and hypocritical. He was rude to and extremely critical of both Rebecca and the kids. He had reverted back to his "Oscar the Grouch" days. His wife didn't know what to do. She tried to talk to him several times, but he only withdrew. To make matters worse, he threw himself into his work and was rarely available to his family.

Although their first few years together were good, by 1996, the marriage was in absolute disarray. What happened? Tragically and as occurs all too often, they failed to address a treatable infection when it was first diagnosed, thus allowing it to metastasize and infiltrate every aspect of the relationship. The ailment was bitterness. Rob thought he had conquered the emotion in 1981, but it had resurfaced. He knew that as a Christian he was to be joyful, but he wasn't.

Extremely self-conscious and a bit immature, Rob exacerbated the problem through his inability to separate himself from it. Rebecca had had a relationship during their engagement that caused Rob a great deal of envy. The other man had become, in Rob's mind, the standard by which Rebecca would judge him. But instead of getting the issue out in the open, he tried to ignore it. Regardless, it hounded Rob for the next two decades. The foundation was laid for what would be a slow but steady decline in the relationship.

Rebecca reached the point of despair in 1997. At a loss, she decided to reach out to her husband via a letter in which she poured out her heart, describing in great detail the monster he had become.

Rob knew things weren't great. Prior to perusing the letter, however, he had no idea of the intense pain Rebecca felt. It caught him off guard and left him angry, although he directed the rage primarily at himself. He was culpable and therefore couldn't refute any of his wife's allegations. He had been and continued to be all of the things listed in her letter. As tough as it was to read Rebecca's words, this was a defining moment for him. He saw for the first time what he had become, and it tore him up inside.

Rob genuinely wanted to change, but he didn't. For reasons that only recently became clear to him, the harder he tried, the worse things got. It was as if he were handcuffed and forced down this evil path, kicking and fighting the entire way. His situation was akin to that described in Romans 7:15: "For I am not practicing what I would like to do, but I am doing the very thing I hate." Why wasn't God changing him? Just like he had as a teenager, Rob turned his frustrations into anger against the Lord.

The situation, as frustrating as it was, became highly ironical. The harder he sought joy, the less he found: God was cheating him all over again. Once more, he fled the Lord, blaming Him for the problems that his own faithlessness created. This time, however, he wasn't the only casualty of the misdirected anger. His wife and kids would end up absorbing a large portion of the blow.

To complicate matters, Rob lost his business in 1998. He

had been selling educational software from an office in his house to those who home-schooled their children. He enjoyed his work very much and felt that it was the one thing he was doing that served God. Unfortunately, it did not provide him a decent living, and he had to find alternate employment. This made him question God even more. Why would He eliminate a ministry that glorified His name? Rob's loss just added fuel to the fire, propelling him towards an even more severe depression.

Rather than try to start up another business from home, he decided to seek outside employment. Not only would outside work provide a better opportunity to earn a good salary, it would also get him away from his wife. He could no longer handle being around her for long stints. The guilt was overwhelming.

Rob had heard of a job opening through a friend at church. It was a sales position and with Rob's gregarious personality, he would do well. The problem was that he had become very lazy and irresponsible and rarely followed through on anything.

God's timing is amazing. He placed in Rob's life just the man he needed at that particular moment. His new boss tolerated no indolence; he resembled a boot camp drill sergeant more than a sales manager. As Rob likes to say, "I jumped out of the frying pan—my home—and into the fire." God did to Rob what He had done to Jonah. When we run from Him, He turns up the heat.

It wouldn't take long before Rob's boss was reprimanding him. But rather than get defensive, he took all that was thrown at him. Seeing each tirade as an opportunity, he would return to his desk and pray that it not be wasted on him. Rob knew that God had put this man in his life for a reason. It was to purify him. To his chagrin, the purifying agent came in the form of fire: if he was going to change, Rob first needed to be refined in God's crucible. This would be the only way the "dross" or impurities could be purged from his soul. His boss filled the role of flame quite nicely. The "chewing out" sessions continued for two long years. Rob freely admits that he had it coming each and every time. In fact, his performance, at least initially, probably warranted termination. Each time his boss threatened to let him go, Rob remained stoic and withstood the heat. They could fire him, but he wasn't going to quit. He was committed to changing. Rob did see some growth; however, this was just the beginning of what would be a rough and hilly road.

Rob would stay on for two additional years before being laid off in December of 2001. Due to the impending bankruptcy of his employer, he once again found himself out of work. It was no accident: God was ready to implement the next step in purification. This time, however, He would use a much hotter flame—his wife. Rob was forced to return to the very place from which he was trying to escape.

Rebecca didn't scream and yell like his former boss—it wasn't necessary. For the four months he was unemployed and at home, she would simply be Rob's mirror. Through her, he would see reflections of his true self.

They were certainly not pretty. He hated what he saw and tried to avoid "the mirror" at all costs. As the months passed, exposing additional angles of his physiognomy, Rob continued to retreat. And God had had enough. To break him, He zoomed in still further on Rob, revealing every crevice of his ugliness. The revelation hit him hard. It was as if he had just been run over by a truck—as if his face had been splattered on its grill.

Rob's grief took on new meaning. While he had always been remorseful, he now began to agonize and weep over the person he had become. This was monumental, for he hadn't shed a tear in years. He began to fervently fast and pray over the marriage. In fact, he felt compelled to reach out publicly to his wife. And in September of 2002, in front of a packed church congregation, Rob read a letter to Rebecca outlining his offenses and seeking her forgiveness. He was truly sorry.

Now more than ever, he was determined to change. Rob was confident. With God's assistance, real progress seemed possible. As before, however, there was no headway. His errant behavior continued almost without interruption. Rebecca was hurt and dismayed. She had been so hopeful that this would be the turning point for her husband.

What Rob had failed to understand was that his sorrow, while sincere, came from the head, not the heart. God wanted him to be more than just apologetic and contrite. Rob didn't comprehend it at the time, but the Lord wanted him completely and unequivocally empty.

But he wasn't. Consequently, blessing was denied. His earnest prayers that Rebecca experience his love and that he become a better father and husband were refused. Rob kept hearing God say, "No, I cannot use you." And he hurt. These were biblical prayers. Why wouldn't He answer them? (Rob had misheard Him. God's response wasn't, "No." It was, "Not yet.") The harder he tried, the worse things became. He was caught in a vicious cycle that left him absolutely bewildered.

Deflated, Rob began praying a different prayer. If God wasn't going to change him, he wanted to be taken home to Heaven. He knew that neither suicide nor divorce was an option. Yet he had to save his family from himself. If Rob was unable to be the husband God needed him to be, Rebecca was better off without him. God again said no. The misery only worsened.

It wasn't until March of 2003, while he was reading Hosea 10:2, that his eyes began to open, albeit slightly. He knew, at least intellectually, that his affections were divided between Rebecca and God and that the division was harming his relationship with both. However, he failed to understand not only the severity of the problem but also the simplicity of the solution. God is a jealous god and demands that we pursue His love with greater passion than anyone else's, including our spouses'. Rob was seeking in marriage what could only be found in Him. He and Rebecca both paid a price for it.

God also demands that we surrender to His sovereignty, not merely seek His assistance. The Lord wasn't interested in being Rob's subordinate or in receiving his aid. God's will manifests itself in a manner and in an hour of His choosing. When we try to intervene, despair becomes inevitable.

In speaking with Chuck, Rob learned that if he was ever to experience joy, he needed to be in desperation, not despair. There is a big difference between the two. In fact, they are in diametrical opposition. Despair is an outlook dictated by the confines of a circumstance. Desperation is an outlook engendered by hope *despite* the confines of that circumstance; it suggests a readiness to move towards unconditional submission to Jesus Christ.

Because Rob had failed to relinquish power, he was unable to take his pain to the cross and unload it there. At a loss, he chose to bottle up the misery and cork the bottle; the repression rendered him emotionally and spiritually bankrupt.

With the help of Chuck and his counseling partner, Jerome, Rob realized that he was repeating the pattern he was in twenty years ago in relation to his height—he was harboring deep anger. God broke that bottle, allowing him to experience emotion again. More than just another purging was needed. It was now time for Rob to break out of his confines by forfeiting control.

He went home and spent that September night on his knees. Rob again prayed that God either take him or change him. He cried out, "If I am willing to die for the benefit of family, why can't I live for them? Let me live for them, Lord!"

He expressed his desperation in a journal. The text is long but well worth printing in its entirety. It accounts for the emotional anguish Rob was facing and provides a prelude to the miracle that would ensue moments later.

I must weep. I must weep enough tears with deep enough sorrow and grieving to break the bottle in which I have confined myself. I thought I was safe. I thought I was protected—protected from the pain. The pain of distant memories. One set of memories of long ago which seemed from another lifetime. Memories of pain—deep, deep emotional pain of being so small. The pain of having the life I longed for ripped away from me. Going into the bottle, becoming invisible. And then another set of memories. The bottle breaking and becoming visible once again. Memories of joy, love, and finally, a oneness like never before with someone. The oneness that had previously been only a fantasy in a dream—longed for, ached for. And until then, never obtained. But the dream that had now become a reality had a shadow. A shadow holding a nightmare that was always at the edge of the dream. The nightmare was the specter of a past. A past that held the greatest treasure that would never be mine.

In the light I lived. For a while, the fantasy and the dream were real. But the light faded away. The wind of the troubles of the day blew on the dream. And at some point the dream was over. It wasn't the first set of memories that started building the bottle—memories of the pain from my childhood due to being so small. It was a second set of memories of the way our friendship and marriage had been. The wall grew. Grew as the memories came. Because the memories hurt. Not from revisiting old wounds, like the first set of memories. The other memories hurt because they too had become nightmares. Specters of what was longed for, in what once was, but now is no more. So now two sets of nightmares are haunting. The one of what once was, but now is no more. The other of a treasure of greatest passion and desire that will forever belong to someone else—a specter of her past.

And so the wall grew ever thicker to protect me from the dual pains. But alas, the reality is that there is no protection—no more than a clear glass bottle protects from light or darkness. For the dual pains sandwiched me in the middle, squeezing out the good things in me. And I hated the empty shell that was left of me! So the bottle now became a prison.

And I cried out to God.

His answer: "I have a purpose; I have a will. Although you cannot see it, maybe someday you shall. And in that purpose, and in that will, it is what it is. The treasure will never be yours. As for making what once was into 'once again'—that remains to be seen."

Until then, I remain the dry, empty shell.

God demanded that Rob completely empty himself. Pure refinery required that the only reflection in him be his Maker's. God wanted nothing that might taint the blessing to come. He wanted and rightly deserved the glory all for Himself. There would be no shred of Rob left to steal any acclaim.

The reality of God's complete sovereignty began to melt Rob's hardened heart. The fact that he needed to forfeit control and make God everything and himself nothing began to sink in and touch his soul. He prayed that the Lord take the reins. He also implored, with great humility, that God make him the husband and father he should be but had never been. After a river of tears, the Holy Spirit interceded. He told Rob, "You are ready. And I will." God changed him in a flash. What Rob took two decades to erect, God destroyed in a second. The bottle shattered. It was an absolute miracle. Overwhelmed with joy and gratitude, Rob added these thoughts to his journal:

> Praise be to God, for He has filled my empty shell with His spirit that I may live for Him. Praise be to God, that He will love Rebecca through me, like I will never be able to love her on my own—unconditionally.

It was an incredible night. Dying to self is a wonderful thing. God had just crucified Rob's carnal nature and given this hopeless man true life. He wrote these last lines the next morning:

> I can only truly live when I die. Die to me, die to self. It is not I who live, but Christ who lives in me and through me. And as for love, I may die to love too. And die to my need to be "loved" by Rebecca. For if I truly die to self and to my need for Rebecca's love then I can truly live, for Christ can now truly live in me. And through me. For I need not Rebecca's love. What I really need is Christ to live in me and through me. And for Christ to love Rebecca through me.

Chuck later pointed out how this truth underlines that related in Galatians 2:20: "I have been crucified with Christ; and it is no longer I who live, but Christ lives in me; and the life which I now live in the flesh I live by faith in the Son of God, who loved me, and delivered Himself up for me."

He had to tell Rebecca the news. Unfortunately, she wasn't home at the time. Under the pretext of a family vacation, he had two weeks earlier shipped his wife and kids off to Florida. In reality, he selfishly wanted to be by himself and away from everyone else.

When Rob called her and shared the events of the night before, Rebecca's tone was reserved and her response measured. She had heard this from him before. Her reply was, in essence, "Don't tell me, show me." Oh how she prayed that this would be a true transformation.

It would take some time, but Rebecca did see real, albeit gradual, change. Rob's sour attitude and sharp tongue began to diminish and were replaced by words of encouragement and edification. She was getting a taste of Ephesians 5:25: "Husbands, love your wives, just as Christ also loved the church and gave Himself up for her."

Their love for each other, with God as the conduit, grew far deeper than what they could have ever manufactured on their own. It greatly exceeded their expectation. Because it was channeled through Him and not them, the couple availed themselves of a love far truer.

Though he had read 1 Corinthians 13 many times, Rob finally started to internalize the significance of verses 4-7. "Love is patient, love is kind, and is not jealous; love does not brag and is not arrogant, does not act unbecomingly; it does not seek its own, is not provoked, does not take into account a wrong suffered, does not rejoice in unrighteousness, but rejoices with the truth; bears all things, believes all things, hopes all things, endures all things."

Rob did not learn until six months after his transformation

the previous September that Rebecca had also been praying that God show His love to her. He answered both of their prayers and did so through a most unexpected source—Rob himself. With the Lord as his guide, Rob no longer had to worry about competing with ghosts from the past. He now had the very Author of love in his corner. Since he was now free to love his wife as God intended, the jealousy that once consumed him vanished.

Rob's refining continues yet today with regard to his children. While their relationships have improved, there is still much lost ground to recover. He prays that the Lord will do yet another wonderful work in him. Having become a vehicle through which Rebecca feels her Maker's love, Rob hopes to fill that same role vis-à-vis his children.

Rob recently gave his testimony at a Rebuilders meeting. It was a powerful hour. God has performed a true miracle in this man's life. And given the ear-to-ear grin Rebecca wore the entire night, it's safe to say that she wholeheartedly agrees.

After he finished his remarks, we fittingly sang *Rejoice in the Lord*. It's a strong testament to God's patience and mercy.

> God never moves without purpose or plan
> When trying His servant and molding a man.
> Give thanks to the Lord though your testing seems
>   long;
> In darkness He giveth a song.
>
> Chorus:
> O rejoice in the Lord, He makes no mistake.
> He knoweth the end of each path that I take.
> For when I am tried and purified,
> I shall come forth as gold.

I could not see through the shadows ahead;
So I looked at the cross of my Savior instead.
I bowed to the will of the Master that day;
Then peace came and tears fled away.

Now I can see testing comes from above;
God strengthens His children and purges in love.
My Father knows best, and I trust in His care;
Through purging more fruit I will bear.[11]

11

Finding the Real Jesus

Raised in a home where piety was mere rule keeping, Lisa saw firsthand the folly inherent in maintaining meaningless religious ritual. While caring and loving, her parents were more concerned with outward appearance than inward purity. Sunday mornings consisted of donning nice clothes and warming pew seats. Church was a glorified social hour.

Tragically, church teaching and biblical reality don't necessarily always mean the same thing. It's dangerous to presume they do. There is an ever-expanding gap between the Jesus of the Bible and the Jesus depicted in many mainstream congregations. Rather than exalted and treasured, Christ is being marginalized or completely ignored.

A continuum of misguided theology drives the errant preaching. On one end is the ugly head of legalism with its smothering, grace-robbing "to do" lists; on the other is the anarchy of licentiousness where the lists are discarded but replaced with feel-good, self-help manuals. Parishioners are either told how to perform "religion" or encouraged to create their own. In either extreme, Christ is made small and treated as if insignificant. We seek Him when it's convenient and not too intrusive, turning worship service into an uninspiring and inconsequential, though well-orchestrated, display of human labor. Without the Savior, that's all it can ever hope to be.

Experience has taught me that those exposed to such dreadful circumstances typically follow one of three general paths: become misled and practice a fruitless faith, become skeptical and seek truth elsewhere, or become indifferent and go into spiritual exile. Lisa fell into the last category. Though she wouldn't articulate such reservation until after leaving home, seeing Jesus Christ through the lens of a dead church had a profound impact on her spirituality. How could it not?

After all she had (or hadn't) seen, Lisa was left unimpressed and had no desire to play the game. What value was there in pursuing a valueless God? Not realizing that a more dynamic and powerful Christ existed, she turned her back and walked away from organized religion.

This apathy slowly evolved into cynicism while she was at college. She was an international relations major and spent much time studying the poverty and tremendous suffering in underdeveloped nations. As she did so, her preeminent question became not whether God mattered but whether He even existed. Lisa was tinkering on the edge of atheism.

As the years progressed, she would sway back and forth between uncertainty, complacency, and flat-out disbelief. For all of the confusion, though, Lisa never came to a final verdict on a God she wanted to believe existed. It was as if she were waiting for Him to provide a hook upon which to hang a hat of hope.

Lisa married in 1988. She had met her husband, Adam, in a nightclub six years earlier. Though the two did attend church, they were, for all intents and purposes, just going through the motions as her parents had. The irony would have been comical if it hadn't been so sad.

Lisa's waywardness would not continue on indefinitely, however. In 1993, an event took place that would forever change her worldview and bring to an end this long-standing malaise. It was the miracle of birth. Through her beautiful baby boy, she began to see that, in her words, "There was more to me than me." The most important person in Lisa's life was now no longer Lisa—she gladly surrendered that honor. With the shift in focus came the insight that reality might not be as random and disconnected as she previously thought. There appeared to be a design and purpose behind it. In hindsight, this realization was the first step in her journey towards finding the real Jesus.

Just when her life seemed to be taking on greater significance, however, Lisa was dealt a serious blow. Her husband confessed to adultery. Though she was unsure how long he had been unfaithful, Adam promised to end the promiscuity and attend counseling. Unfortunately, the assistance wasn't grounded in biblical truth and had no appreciable impact on either of them.

Despite the inadequate counsel, the couple was able to reassemble some of the broken pieces. Though they hadn't sufficiently resolved their issues, Lisa sacrificially stuffed the anger and hurt into the far recesses of her heart so that they could move forward as a family. And by most standards, they functioned surprisingly well.

Some six years later, however, Adam resumed his pursuit of other women. He would tell Lisa, as if to justify his behavior, that she was a wonderful mother but a terrible wife. Growing tired of his responsibilities at home, he eventually packed up and moved out. Deeply hurt, Lisa managed the pain by doting on her son. Since she didn't know Christ, he was the only release she had.

She didn't give up on the marriage, though. Lisa was able to convince Adam to join her for additional counseling.

Unfortunately, it too proved fruitless. After only a few sessions, it became readily apparent that her husband was no longer interested in reconciliation. He had moved on not only physically but now also emotionally. At a loss, the pastor providing the counsel gave Lisa unbiblical instruction. She was to give Adam an ultimatum: either end the current affair and move back home or be served divorce papers. Even though she had no intention of actually following through, Lisa issued the threat. Adam didn't even flinch.

Recognizing that he wasn't going to return, she began to prepare herself for life without him. The first step was to begin, if not accepting, at least acknowledging the pain Adam had caused. As Lisa began replaying in her head the difficult history, the floodgates unexpectedly flung open and a decade's worth of suppressed emotion came rushing through. She became inundated with one painful memory after another.

As hard as each was to relive, the post-mortem was necessary. It enabled her to more objectively investigate why the union had become so strained and—of particular significance—what role she played in its demise. This gave Lisa a sense of closure and allowed her to move forward. There was, however, an additional, more important benefit to the exercise. It forced this woman to begin revisiting preconceived notions about both the origin and remission of sin—and her own in particular.

Until this point, she had always understood transgressions to be relative in nature. Some were worse than others. It all depended upon the severity. As sinners go, Lisa was doing okay. She had never committed any egregious acts against God. Hers were all misdemeanors.

Lisa's spiritual relativism reduced the Lord, in effect, to a bean counter. Salvation was an accounting tabulation. The key was, if on the off chance He actually existed, to keep her bank account with Him in the black. If she could stay away from the large debits and muster up enough good works to cancel out the periodic blemishes, things would be just fine. This balance sheet approach afforded Lisa the luxury of thinking she controlled her own destiny.

This theology came under heavy scrutiny in the months following the post-mortem, however. Though spiritual interrogation was nothing new for her, this particular inquiry was different. Unbeknownst to Lisa at the time, it was of supernatural origin. God had stepped in and with great care softened her heart. And she yielded. Rather than run from the Lord, as she had so often in the past, Lisa began walking towards Him in the fall of 2000.

Not yet saved and in need of the Gospel, the Lord led her to Rebuilder Ministries. She had heard of it while attending another outreach group.

Under Chuck's guidance, Lisa learned that she was measuring her virtue against the wrong standard. Her gauge needed to be God, not other people. As she made the necessary adjustments, a couple of key truths came to light: one, she was a sinner in dire need of rescue; and two, the Rescuer was a glorious Savior offering not only redemption but also great joy. The pair of discoveries served important but distinct functions. The first drove Lisa to the cross; the second kept her there.

Discarding the Jesus of her youth and with him decades of futility and confusion, Lisa embraced the Jesus of the Bible. She took Him as her Savior by faith alone. "And without faith it is impossible to please Him, for he who comes to God must believe that He is, and that He is a rewarder of those who seek Him" (Hebrews 11:6). Oh, how glorious it was that she was finally able to break through the muck and find the true Christ.

Although she was saved, her problems didn't necessarily go away, however. In fact, some of them, particularly those involving her marriage, actually worsened. Adam pressed for divorce in the winter of 2001. Against Lisa's wishes, the union ended the following spring. He would remarry just three months later.

Though sad, Lisa considered herself blessed. She banked on God's promise in Joshua 1:9: "Have I not commanded you? Be strong and courageous! Do not tremble or be dismayed, for the Lord your God is with you wherever you go." She realized that peace is not dependent upon God changing life events; it's a result of taking comfort in the fact that our Maker is in complete control, in both good times and bad. If your delight is contingent upon an affliction-free existence, you have not fully availed yourself of God's grace. For if you had, you would know that some of the deepest joys in life come during seasons of trouble.

God provided Lisa the strength not only to endure the pain but also to prosper in the midst of it. The Lord told Paul in 2 Corinthians, "My grace is sufficient for you, for power is perfected in weakness." Paul's response:

> Most gladly, therefore, I will rather boast about my weaknesses, that the power of Christ may dwell in me. Therefore I am well content with weaknesses, with insults, with distresses, with persecutions, with difficulties, for Christ's sake; for when I am weak, then I am strong (12:9-10).

Strength through weakness seems counterintuitive. I know of no coach who extols muscular atrophy as the first step towards proper conditioning. Yet that is exactly what God commands of us in order that we achieve spiritual fitness. It's not muscle that must shrink, but pride. Before we can avail ourselves of God's blessing and become strong in Him, we must first whither and make weak our carnal propensity to self-exalt. There's only one King, and it isn't you or I. Until we crack that facade and see ourselves for what we truly are—weak and broken sinners—we will be precluded from consuming the nutrients a strong faith requires.

The cycle is a glorious one. In very simplified terms, here's how I believe it works: Weakness (brokenness) leads to humility as we realize that answers lie outside of self. Humility leads to knowledge as we strip away ego, allowing truth to penetrate our thinking. Knowledge leads to desperation as we comprehend both the temporal and eternal consequences of continuing to rely upon our own finite resources. Desperation leads to faith as we gain exposure to the infinite power of Christ. Faith leads to strength as we prosper from God's abundant grace, regardless of circumstance.

What a tremendous blessing it is to become weak. It all begins with understanding your condition and coming to terms with who you are and who you are not. Through God's mercy, Lisa made that distinction and consequently found the real Jesus. She has been reaping the benefits ever since.

12

Filling the Void

As most girls do growing up, Beth dreamt of having a fairy tale life. She would find the perfect man, get married, have kids, and live happily ever after. For anyone who has ever dared to dream, things don't necessarily always go the way we envision, however. God more times than not has a different path for us. He certainly did for Beth.

The first of what would be many detours came in 1985. Beth, just ten years old, became the victim of a molestation. Unable to understand the event, she said nothing. Though she knew deep down that what had happened was wrong, fear and confusion kept her from taking any action.

Two years later, she was dealt another blow. A family friend murdered her father and severely beat her mother. Understandably, this Christian home went into a tailspin. Extremely distraught, Beth was unable to reach out and provide any form of comfort to her mother, brother, or sister, nor they to her. As she put it, "We were lost in our own misery."

As if that weren't enough, Beth faced additional

unsolicited sexual advances as her teenage years came to a close. In each case, her aggressor brainwashed her into believing that the encroachments were actually her own fault: Beth had brought them on by walking, talking, and dressing so provocatively. Believing the lie and not wanting to cause further disruption, she again said nothing.

This notion that she was to blame for the aggression, a fiction that had followed her since she was a young teenager, had a huge impact on Beth. She began to feel as though she was worthy of nothing more than a man's lust—certainly not his love. Such was her self-image, as baseless as it was. When you hear a lie from enough sources, whether credible or not, eventually you begin, if not believing, at least entertaining the possibility that it might be accurate. In either case, you obligate yourself to research the claim and locate evidence that will refute it.

Beth set out to do just that. She would spend the next ten years trying to invalidate the assertions hurled at her the prior seven. She would go from relationship to relationship, searching for the man that would not only rescue her from the past, but also, more importantly, prove that she was indeed worthy of someone's love. (A part of her still clung to a small glimmer of hope that she could fulfill that childhood dream of living "happily ever after.") He had to exist, she reasoned. It was just a matter of crossing his path.

Finding a sustainable love was doable. Beth, however, simply became confused as to where to look. She would seek in man what could only be obtained through Christ. Rather than run to God, she ran from Him. Consequently, her life became a chronology of one futile and reckless attempt after another to fill the void. The situation was highly ironic: her efforts to escape the pain only produced more of it, layering unnecessary misery on top of an already dismal past.

Her running produced a second consequence, though. When we turn from God and His Word, we are less immune to spiritual attack. We become susceptible to the lies the world and Satan would have us believe. Beth, as fragile and impressionable as she was given the emotional baggage she already carried, was an ideal target.

This certainly played itself out in what would be the first leg of her self-guided journey. As she skipped from one man to another, a pattern began to develop. She had a certain propensity to attract men who were interested primarily in one thing, and it wasn't her happiness. With each failed attempt at love, the small glimmer of hope of finding Mr. Right faded. After two years of grueling, fruitless searching, Beth reached what appeared, at least to her, to be an inevitable conclusion—she was, in fact, unlovable. Satan had Beth right where he wanted her.

Deflated and dejected, Beth resigned hope of ever attracting a decent man and stopped looking. She couldn't shoulder any more disappointment. She was done with dating. For a year and a half, she stayed true to her word and didn't even contemplate it.

That all changed, however, the day Timothy walked into her life. The big and lovable bear caught her attention the first time she laid eyes on him. This man intrigued Beth. He seemed different from the others. Proceeding with great caution, she made the effort to become better acquainted.

One thing led to another and they ended up going on a date. He was a great listener and a lot of fun to be around. He was not only polite and kind-hearted but also genuinely devoted to God. To put it mildly, Beth was pleased with how the date went. It was certainly a nice departure from the past.

The two hit it off, and their relationship developed quickly. She felt both alive and secure when they were together. In fact, things progressed so nicely that Beth thought she might have finally found the right man. Perhaps her dream of running off into the sunset hand-in-hand was possible after all.

The two became engaged in December of 1996 and were married in April of 1997. She could finally put the painful past behind her, for Timothy would be her portion. He would erase the awful past and give her new life.

As it had all too frequently in the past, reality quickly caught up to Beth. Not long after the honeymoon, the long conversations, relaxing walks, and shared moments that were such an integral part of their courtship came to a gradual halt. Timothy, for whatever reason, became disengaged. He was no longer the same man who had swept her off her feet. What had happened?

Now that he had bagged his trophy, he seemed content to allow it to gather dust on the shelf. This was not supposed to happen. Timothy was going to be her fix and provide the peace she had long sought. Beth was beside herself. When she raised her concerns about the growing distance between them, Timothy listened closely, apologized, and promised to do better. The good intent would last for about a week; then he would revert back to his old ways. Though he never intended to hurt Beth, his inability to comprehend the seriousness of the problem and act with some level of urgency only further fueled his wife's anger and frustration.

Timothy's failure to love Beth in a manner she found acceptable sent her once again looking elsewhere for fulfillment. Resourceful as she was, she soon came up with a solution. They would have a child. That would fill the void. Clearly, it was the missing link.

Two children and a ton of frustration later, the hole was bigger than ever. While she loved her kids, she was unable to find satisfaction through them, either. In fact, she found the role incredibly draining. Beth equated it to a Hi C box with ten straws poked into it; everyone was sucking mom dry. She didn't understand it. The women at church always seemed so energetic when around their children. Why wasn't she? The problem must have lain with her—good moms don't have these issues. It was a troubling conclusion to reach and only further exacerbated her already strong sense of worthlessness.

Beth was tired—tired of crying, tired of failing, tired of the fruitless searching. She reached a point where she simply went numb and became indifferent not only to her lofty dreams but to daily life. With few friends and a husband who remained detached, she began isolating herself. She concluded hopelessly that this was going to be her life—a far cry from the fairy tale she had long dreamt of.

Just a few weeks later, Timothy asked if he could bring a coworker home for dinner. Tom was a bachelor, and given the fact that Beth was a great cook, it would be gracious to extend the invitation. She always enjoyed playing the role of host and agreed to have him over. Perhaps a new face would help get her mind off her problems.

After enjoying a wonderful meal, the three sat down in the living room and conversed. They talked for several hours. Beth particularly enjoyed the evening. It was nice to have someone in the house who was willing to engage in adult conversation. She enjoyed Tom's company.

To extend the hospitality, Timothy continued to invite his friend over for supper. His visits grew to become a regular weekly routine. They were becoming the highlight of Beth's week. She found Tom refreshing and appreciated the interest he took in her. He was becoming everything that Timothy no longer was. Before she knew it, she was emotionally attached to him. As her defenses were down, the already ill-advised relationship took a turn for the worse and became a physical one, albeit for a short period of time.

Beth was mortified and overwhelmed with guilt. She didn't know what to do. Part of her blamed Timothy. After all, had he stayed connected, this would never have happened. Through the guidance of a good friend, Beth realized that she needed to confess to her husband.

As the two sat down on the couch, she shared the news. Tears began forming in the corner of Timothy's eyes. With a soft, broken voice he reaffirmed his love for Beth and forgave her unconditionally. He then proceeded to ask for her forgiveness; he clearly had not served or loved her in a manner that was pleasing to God.

Though she was touched, Timothy's response actually made Beth feel even guiltier. Her husband's forgiveness came too easily. It wasn't commensurate with the sin. He should have become outraged. Instead, he seeks her pardon? Someone had to exact proper punishment, Beth thought to herself. She must pay for her actions; otherwise, it would be impossible to find inner peace. She told Timothy to kick her out of the house; she wasn't worthy of being a wife or a mother.

"That is foolish talk," Timothy told her. They would, with Christ at the helm, make it through this. Realizing they needed outside help, the two sought counseling. They had heard of Chuck Raichert through a friend at church and decided to make an appointment.

The woman who walked into Chuck's office for that first visit was completely defeated and entertained thoughts of committing suicide. Beth carried a heavy burden. She felt completely unlovable and unforgivable. She would never be able to move forward, given what she had done. Even if she could, Timothy most likely would revert back to his old ways. She was completely without hope.

Two hours later, she walked out with guarded optimism. What had happened?

Chuck's first task was to show Beth that she was a child of God and therefore privy to His abundant grace and love. If she was sincerely repentant, there was no need to be dragged down by the weight of the past. Christ had conquered her sin at Calvary. He paid the debt once and for all. She owed nothing!

Chuck walked her through Romans 8 with particular emphasis placed on verses 35 and 38-39:

> Who shall separate us from the love of Christ? Shall tribulation, or distress, or persecution, or famine, or nakedness, or peril, or sword? . . . For I am convinced that neither death, nor life, nor angels, nor principalities, nor things present, nor things to come, nor powers, nor height, nor depth, nor any other created thing, shall be able to separate us from the love of God, which is in Christ Jesus our Lord.

Because of the cross, Beth is lovable, and Beth is forgivable. She has a future, and it's all because of Jesus Christ.

His second task was to persuade her that she had been seeking happiness in all the wrong places. Timothy, though he certainly needed to change, would never be her portion. Even if he were the godliest man on earth, he still would be ill-equipped to fulfill the role. To expect otherwise is to invite what is certain disappointment. The same applied to her children. Don't misread: a godly spouse and beautiful children are tremendous blessings. However, when they become the source of our joy rather than a channel for it, we set ourselves up for tremendous heartache. Beth's peace was contingent upon the ability of other human beings, as fallible and unreliable as they may be, to produce events from which she could extract a tolerable existence. Her situation was a disaster in the making. The only true source of life-preserving joy is Jesus!

For Timothy, the message was simple. He needed to love his wife as God intended. He was not meeting his end of the bargain. God gave Beth to him, Chuck conveyed, for a purpose: to care for her as Christ cared for the Church. This included being more emotionally accessible. Beth needed him to be connected.

Both individuals took home hope that day—hope that they could let go of the past and build a brighter future together. Chuck gave each of them their respective assignments. Timothy needed to learn to dispense love, and Beth to accept it.

A couple of weeks passed and Timothy, who is typically a very sound sleeper, suddenly awoke in the middle of the night. God had put on his heart the need to write his wife a letter. With pen in hand, he sat down at the kitchen table and poured out his thoughts on paper. A portion of the letter appears below. He titled it *My Crown*. It is based on Proverbs 12:4: "An excellent wife is the crown of her husband."

> I offer up this prayer to God our Father, our faithful and loving God in everything we face. I know that I must trust you with the greatest gift you ever gave me—my wife, my beloved crown, the queen of my home. I must trust you, Lord, with this good woman. This woman who has brought me enough joy for a thousand lifetimes. This woman who has given me so much love that I could never repay it in a million years. This precious woman—this precious, precious woman. This virtuous woman that I have been so blessed to have, Lord. I don't know why you chose me, or how you could ever have trusted me with this most precious gem on earth. Or how, God, you ever thought I was worthy of such an awesome responsibility. How you, God, ever thought I could be even a portion or a fraction of all she is to me. I don't understand it, but I have been so blessed. This girl is my everything. This Beth is my everything. So Lord, hold her in your strong arms, I pray. I wrote that I don't know why you blessed me or how you could have trusted me with this gift, with worth far above that of precious gems or diamonds. I still don't know

why God, but I thank you. I thank you for all the lessons learned, for all the fun had, for all the joy-filled times, for all the love shared. For these things are all I can remember: the joy, the love, the fun, the important lessons learned. I am so blessed to know this priceless jewel. Thank you, God, for all that you have given me in her. She has never wronged me, she has never hurt me, there has never been a time that I have felt unloved by her. She has never failed me, she has never cheated me, she has never been selfish toward me, she has never been unfaithful to me, she has always put me second only to Christ who is her first. Thank you, God, thank you, for this unwavering woman who has never, ever, not even one time, done me wrong. Despite all my shortcomings, and all the reasons I would have given her, and in all my failure, she has remained true. She is faithful; she is noble. How God could I ever thank you enough?

After reading the letter, Beth cried and asked how he could possibly have written such words. They weren't true, she argued. She had wronged him; she had failed him. Timothy, who knew his own wicked heart, responded humbly that through Christ the slate is wiped clean. Each day is a fresh start, as we are made anew. As far as God was concerned, Beth had a spotless record. To believe otherwise would be to play right into Satan's deceiving hands. For the repentant Christian, the past is just that.

So that it might serve as a daily reminder of God's great gift to him, Timothy had the letter framed; it hangs on their living room wall. Heeding Chuck's counsel, he has spent the last two years validating for Beth through word and action that everything he wrote is true. In a sense, he has been courting her all over again. He found both guidance and encouragement in Psalm 34:4-9:

> I sought the Lord, and He answered me, and delivered me from all my fears. They looked to Him and were radiant, and their faces shall never be ashamed. This poor man cried and the Lord heard him; and saved him out of all his troubles. The angel of the Lord encamps around those who fear Him, and rescues them. O taste and see that the Lord is good; how blessed is the man who takes refuge in Him! O fear the Lord, you His saints; for to those who fear Him, there is no want.

He also leaned on James 1:2-4: "Consider it all joy, my brethren, when you encounter various trials, knowing that the testing of your faith produces endurance. And let endurance have its perfect result, that you may be perfect and complete, lacking in nothing."

Beth has made great strides towards understanding the significance of what Christ did 2,000 years ago and the freedom that we can enjoy because of it. There are times still where doubt and guilt reenter her thinking. She knows that they are not biblical in nature and that she must, through Christ, shield herself from them. She has found 2 Corinthians of great aid towards this end:

> For though we walk in the flesh, we do not war according to the flesh, for the weapons of our warfare are not of the flesh, but divinely powerful for the destruction of fortresses. We are destroying speculations and every lofty thing raised up against the knowledge of God, and we are taking every thought captive to the obedience of Christ (10:3-5).

Beth has learned to hold captive and destroy the thoughts that are not of God. As she continues to gain strength in Christ, the task becomes easier, for Satan will eventually lose interest. He knows when he is outmatched.

God put on Timothy's heart another person who needed his forgiveness—Tom. God commands us to forgive as we have been forgiven. "For in the way you judge, you will be judged; and by your standard of measure, it shall be measured to you" (Matthew 7:2). In obedience to Scripture, Timothy went to Tom a couple weeks after first learning of the affair. What better picture of Christ's forgiveness than Timothy following suit and reaching out to this man who had betrayed him! Timothy communicated that he knew what had happened, but that he forgave Tom. He also shared with Tom that he needed a Savior—one that could relieve him from his unspoken burdens.

Though his words fell on deaf ears, Timothy kept witnessing to Tom at work. In fact, he invited him to a Promise Keepers meeting, which they attended. After it was over, the two headed to a restaurant to talk. Timothy opened the Word to his friend and shared what Christ had done in his own life.

Tom never sought Timothy's forgiveness for his betrayal; nonetheless, Timothy had peace. Any anger or frustration that he might have had towards this man was alleviated the day Timothy forgave him. Jesus was now bearing it, providing Timothy the freedom to focus on other things.

Today, Timothy and Beth have a healthy relationship. Their marriage is a strong testimony to the power of biblical reconciliation. While it is not always perfect, they know that through Christ there is no such thing as an insurmountable obstacle. Reflecting back on the previous couple of years, Timothy wrote the following:

> I am not my own, for I was bought at a price. If He who is my Owner and Master has a different plan for me, who am I to complain or get angry? For I have

learned that through the difficult times, He is molding me into the person He wants me to be. Praise God, even though I have a long way to go.

If you find yourself running from God, please stop and take a moment to catch your breath, but then turn around and head back toward Him. Many people have traveled down your current path. Learn from their stories and avoid unnecessary misery. Whether your source of happiness is money, people, food, or what have you, you will never find satisfaction. Forgo these insatiable desires and fill the void with the only true source of peace and contentment—Jesus Christ.

13

To Die is Gain—
Coming Full Circle

There is perhaps no better way to close these testimonies to Christ's glory than by coming full circle and returning to Chuck's relationship with his father, Charles.

Verbally abusive and emotionally detached during Chuck's youth, his father continued to live a life of indifference and self-reliance. Chuck had witnessed to him numerous times but to no avail. While he was glad his son had found peace, Charles himself saw little need to accept Christ as Lord. He believed each individual needed to rely upon their own understanding of eternity and had no plans to incorporate Jesus into his.

Regrettably, the topic was becoming increasingly contentious between the two men. In fact, it reached the point where Charles, if sensing the issue was about to be raised, would simply hold out his hand like a traffic cop and halt the conversation. Though frustrated, Chuck had no choice but to pull back and hand over the burden to God.

It wasn't until some five years later—when, interestingly enough, conviction landed not on Charles but Chuck—that things began to change. He was attending an evening seminar on forgiveness when the Lord placed on his heart the need to reach out to his father and seek reconciliation. But the issue did not involve their dispute over "religion." God had in mind a matter with a much deeper history.

Chuck had been extremely disobedient toward his father growing up. Not only did he refuse to listen or obey; he had blatantly undermined Charles' authority. Oh, how he had violated Ephesians 6:1-3: "Children, obey your parents in the Lord, for this is right. HONOR YOUR FATHER AND MOTHER (which is the first commandment with a promise), THAT IT MAY BE WELL WITH YOU, AND THAT YOU MAY LIVE LONG ON THE EARTH."

Though he knew full well that his behavior was deplorable, pride and a general oblivion to the effects of unforgiven sin kept him from reconciling with his father. It wasn't until he was sitting in on the seminar that he became aware of the residual damage his inaction was causing. Feeling led to speak to Charles yet that night, he drove to his parents' house after the class. As he suspected, his father was sitting at the kitchen table drinking coffee, smoking a cigarette, and working on a crossword puzzle. It was a routine he had followed for as long as Chuck could remember.

Before Charles had a chance to speak, Chuck sat down and poured out his soul, listing the many ways he hadn't afforded him the proper respect, either as a teenager or as a young adult. After outlining all his offenses and admitting that he should have approached him a long time ago, Chuck asked Charles point-blank for his forgiveness.

Touched and a bit taken back, he remained silent for a moment and then responded with tears in his eyes, "I want to meet the God that would make you come and ask for forgiveness." It was the first time he had seen his father cry. Chuck opened in prayer and, just a few short moments later, Charles invited Jesus into his heart, right there at the kitchen table.

Chuck was amazed. He had come to seek his father's forgiveness, not secure his salvation. But as Chuck humbled himself, removing the layer of vanity that had draped the relationship, his father suddenly saw Christ revealed in full. The Savior's irresistible appeal had been unveiled, and he had to have Him.

Charles' disposition changed instantly. The tough, impenetrable exterior that had forever characterized his personality was flattened. The sarcasm and razor-sharp remarks gave way to words of empathy and edification. He was a new man in Christ and consequently was able to put on a true heart of compassion and gentleness (Colossians 3:12). It was a miracle.

The conversion came none too soon, however. Charles was diagnosed with a late-staged lung cancer but a couple of weeks later. The prognosis was not good. When told, he quoted Romans 6:23: "For the wages of sin is death, but the free gift of God is eternal life in Christ Jesus our Lord." The news was devastating, but it didn't devastate him. In fact, Charles had peace, for he knew better things were to come. "For to me, to live is Christ, and to die is gain" (Philippians 1:21).

Though the cancer was taking its toll, his father's testimony was unlike anything Chuck had ever seen. Old friends would come to visit, and Charles would start crying. When asked if it was due to the pain, he would respond, "No, it's not the cancer. It's you not knowing Christ." His burden for the unsaved brought him more distress than the disease ravaging his body.

The months that led up to his death brought deep healing for the two men. Chuck finally felt his father's love. When the time came to say goodbye, doing so was much easier since he knew not only that his father would be in heaven, but also that they had made amends before he departed. There would be no regrets.

Though it's been over two decades since Charles' passing, Chuck thinks of him often. The memories that keep coming back are not of the thirty years of division and strife, but of the 190 days of sweet and Christ-exalting fellowship they shared towards the end.

If God can crack open the hardened heart of a man like Charles and make it tender and receptive, He can do the same for you or a loved one. It may take a miracle, but that's okay. We worship a God who has monopolized this very market. Like the Rockefellers and Carnegies, He, too, aims for total control. However, it's not money God is after; it's your heart. He doesn't want to share it with anyone or anything. I invite you to take a leap of faith and hold a going out of business sale. Christ's spilt blood is a more than fair purchase price. You can't afford to reject it.

14

The Simplicity of the Gospel

Perhaps you find yourself desiring the type of joy you've just read about but are unsure of how to obtain it. Becoming a recipient of God's grace is not a complicated process. In fact, it requires only one thing: a tender heart. If you have never given your life to the Lord, I invite you to pore over the biblical principles outlined below.

God's Word states:
Man is a sinner. There is not a single individual, outside of Christ, who has walked the face of this earth and not sinned. "For all have sinned and fall short of the glory of God" (Romans 3:23).

"Falling short" implies two things: one, there is a standard by which we are being judged (the fact that a mark was missed demands that one exists); and two, we have all failed in reaching it.

It is a standard driven by the one measuring stick that will satisfy God's own glory—Himself. God is the benchmark, and He requires nothing less than perfection.

"Therefore you are to be perfect, as your heavenly Father is perfect" (Matthew 5:48). "For whoever keeps the whole law and yet stumbles in one point, he has become guilty of all" (James 2:10).

If you are like I was, you're probably thinking that, relatively speaking, your stumbles have been minor and couldn't possibly constitute any serious level of wrongdoing. Chances are you're not a murderer, adulterer, or car thief. And because you've never committed any of the real "biggies," the reasoning goes, your standing with God must be in good order. After all, you are a far better person than the "misfits" shown handcuffed on the evening news every night, right? It would be prudent to keep reading.

Did you know that the Bible says, "Every one who hates his brother is a murderer" (1 John 3:15)? Have you ever been angry with a sibling? "But I say to you, that every one who looks on a woman to lust for her has committed adultery with her already in his heart" (Matthew 5:28). Have you ever had impure sexual thoughts? "You shall not steal" (Exodus 20:15). Have you ever availed yourself of company resources for personal use (faxing, printing, photocopying . . .)?

Sin is not solely a list of things we do but shouldn't. It also comprises things we should do but don't. While these are numerous, one "should do" stands out in particular. It is to treasure God above *all* else.

As we have seen throughout this book, God doesn't tolerate being supplanted by anyone or anything. But that is exactly what happens when we seek satisfaction apart from Him. This is called idolatry. Whether we worship the god of money, leisure, self, sex, food, or promotion, the net effect is the same. We shove God aside, albeit discreetly, and then shelve Him to make room for that day's deity. Such displacement is a product of our own flesh and an assault on God's glory. "Among them we too all formerly lived in the lusts of our flesh, indulging the desires of the flesh and of the mind, and were by nature children of wrath, even as the rest" (Ephesians 2:3).

The bottom line is that we have an impossible task before us. There is no way, given our propensity to sin, any of us will ever meet the mark God has set. Unfortunately, most people don't see it as such. They are relativists and conveniently use other humans, as finite and weak as we all are, as their barometers.

The reality is that the bundles of feedback are mere false positives. They tell the recipients what they want rather than need to hear, lulling them into believing everything is just fine when in fact it isn't. While good for the ego, such exercises wreak havoc on the soul because they mask our true condition.

Sin, regardless of its context or severity, damages our relationship with God and is a function of our corrupt existence. The question becomes, "What are the eternal consequences of our depravity?"

God is righteous. "Righteousness and justice are the foundation of Thy throne; lovingkindness and truth go before Thee" (Psalm 89:14). God is just and must therefore punish sin. Paul warns of this in 2 Thessalonians: "And these will pay the penalty of eternal destruction, away from the presence of the Lord and from the glory of His power" (1:9). "[T]hese" refers to disobedient sinners like you and me. And there is a price to pay, as Romans 6:23 reiterates: "For the wages of sin is death. . . ."

We have a huge dilemma on our hands. God requires us to be perfect in Him, but none of us even comes close. And this failure, as we have just learned, isn't without consequence. Our rebellious hearts have forced separation from the Lord. And because He is righteous, justice must be served. One would have to conclude, given the verses above, that eternal condemnation (hell) is therefore inevitable.

If this is true, how is it that a Billy Graham, a sinner just like you and me, can claim with absolute certainty that he is exempt from such judgment and heaven-bound? What happened to the gap his sin created?

Jesus Christ is the bridge. Oh how thankful I am that Romans 6:23 is a compound sentence. "For the wages of sin is death, *but* the free gift of God is eternal life in Christ Jesus our Lord." (Emphasis added.)

God loved us so much that He sent His Son, who was perfect and sin-free, to die a substitutional death. "All of us like sheep have gone astray, each of us has turned to his own way; but the Lord has caused the iniquity of us all to fall on Him" (Isaiah 53:6). Jesus bled on the cross to pay the price for your sin and mine. He died our death and bore our indiscretions so as to satisfy God's just need to punish unrighteousness. Christ bridged our canyon of sin, allowing us to be found righteous before our Maker.

I liken it to a courtroom. God is the judge. Jesus is the defense attorney; we are the defendants charged with murder. Without representation, we have no hope of escaping death row. While we deserve punishment (for in this court we truly are guilty), we receive an acquittal. But unlike in a normal trial, the defense helps us escape punishment, not through legal loopholes, but by bearing it Himself.

This is called grace. It is God's blessing on a people who deserve wrath but receive the exact opposite—a pardon.

How do you obtain this pardon?

Faith is the driver. Having faith means believing in Jesus Christ and trusting Him alone for salvation. "Believe in the Lord Jesus, and you shall be saved, you and your household" (Acts 16:31). Jesus said, "I am the way, and the truth, and the life; no one comes to the Father, but through Me" (John 14:6). Claiming Him as Savior is not an intellectual exercise. It's about treasuring and adoring Him for all that He has done for you.

Many people reverse the relationship between good

deeds and God's pardon. They think the former leads to the latter: if you do enough decent things, God will look favorably upon you and grant access to heaven. As we have seen, this is *not* what the Bible teaches. You are justified (saved) through faith alone and consequently produce fruit because of a changed heart. "For by grace you have been saved through faith; and that not of yourselves, it is the gift of God; not as a result of works, that no one should boast" (Ephesians 2:8-9). The motivation shifts from performing works in order to earn favor to doing them gladly and willingly because of the favor. You produce not to become saved but because you are saved. Your actions flow from an outpouring of love for the One who restored you.

It's not enough simply to know this truth, however. You must act upon it. If you truly want to be saved and claim Jesus as Lord, you can receive this gift of eternal life right now. God's grace is available to all who seek it. There isn't a sin that Christ's blood does not cover—not one! If you want to start life anew and experience a joy that only the Savior can offer, I invite you to take that step today.

Suggested Prayer
"Dear God, I am a hopeless sinner who deserves judgment. However, I believe Your Son died on the cross to purchase a place in heaven for me. Please forgive me of my sins, for I repent of them. I now place my trust in Jesus Christ alone for my salvation and ask that He become the treasure of my life. In Jesus' name, Amen."

If you truly desire Jesus as your treasure, your eternal home now rests on this promise: "Truly, truly, I say to you, he who believes has eternal life" (John 6:47). You have just made the most important decision of your life. The Jesus you now hold as Savior will bring you a level of peace never before experienced. "Again therefore Jesus spoke to them, saying, 'I am the light of the world; he who follows Me shall not walk in the darkness, but shall have the light of life'" (John 8:12). He continues, "I am the door; if anyone enters through Me, he shall be saved, and shall go in and out, and find pasture. The thief comes only to steal, and kill, and destroy; I came that they might have life, and might have it abundantly" (10:9-10).

Next Steps
1. Find a Bible-preaching church.
2. Pray. Seek God's face and talk to Him. He wants a personal relationship with you.
3. Read your Bible daily. It is your guide to a joyful life in Christ.
4. Surround yourself with other Christians.
5. Spread the good news to others.

15

A Final Word

Although I'm not someone who typically pays much attention to bumper stickers, one recently caught my eye in a church parking lot. It read, "I love my Jesus." I sat there for a good minute wondering why the "my." Wouldn't "I love Jesus" have sufficed?

After thinking more about it, I realized there was purpose behind the pronoun—a significant purpose. It suggests, beyond mere ownership, a certain possessiveness. Anyone who has ever seen a little girl clench to her chest a doll that is about to be taken from her knows the intensity and passion behind the grip. The object is so adored that when danger looms, its keeper fights back and audibly declares, "This is my doll!"

I wonder how many of us claim Jesus as passionately as the little girl claims the doll? Do we treasure Him as she treasures it? Do we hold onto the Savior for dear life and stand ready to defend when someone threatens to take Him from us? Or do we, when push comes to shove, see Christ as somewhat dispensable and merely hand Him over at the first sign of trouble?

We will never know the infinite value of Christ until we embrace the glory of Christ. We do so by allowing Him to draw us in and completely envelope us with His tender mercy and care, *especially* in the difficult times. The joy is so satisfying that, once found, it will lead the recipient to announce with great passion and a dash of combativeness, "I love my Jesus!"

Because of my Jesus, this book gets written. For without Him, Chuck dies of an overdose, and I never receive the counseling needed to get back on the right track. I, too, have seen some dark days—most of them self-imposed. The sin that drove my misery was contempt for the Lord. He had failed me, and I was angry. This supposedly great Savior either wasn't interested in my problems or was incapable of solving them. It mattered little to me which scenario was true, for they shared the same end result.

I tremble every time I read those last few sentences. What pure wickedness! There is no greater sin than denouncing your Lord and Savior and treating Him as if He were worthless.

This faithlessness and the inevitable despair that resulted were not born overnight. Several years of self-absorption and disobedience had passed before they reared their ugly heads. It was, to say the least, a frightful period.

Curiously, as much as I wanted nothing to do with God, particularly towards the latter half of this ill-fated journey, I still sought Him, albeit through vicarious means. Like a leech who attaches itself to the belly of a fish, I hung on the testimonies of others, hoping their faith would help my own grow. I was but a spectator, expecting somehow to receive the same blessing granted those I passively watched. This strategy didn't work, and I eventually stopped looking altogether.

Thankfully, I had a wife who hadn't given up on her Lord and His ability to transform those who had. She had heard of Chuck through a friend and encouraged me to join her in meeting him. Quite honestly, I didn't think it would do any good. What made this guy any different from the other counselors we had already seen? To appease her, I agreed to go.

Oh how grateful I am that I did. I found that Chuck was indeed different. But it wasn't his extraordinary counseling skills that turned me around. It was his extraordinary Savior that made me take notice. He worships a big God, One that is capable of far more than most other believers expect or think possible.

I had been one of those "other believers." The god I sought wasn't omniscient, omnipresent, and omnipotent. He was ignorant, absent, and weak. If I needed something significant in scope, I relied on myself. God certainly wasn't going to be of help.

Chuck quickly but gently exposed and dispelled my errant thinking. I had it all backwards. Christ was bigger than I and larger than my circumstances. He shared with great passion how the Savior had changed his life. The Lord took Chuck from utter despair to bountiful hope. This was no small feat. It was the work of a powerful force.

Chuck's testimony, quite frankly, astounded me. While it would take time to break my hardened heart, his story helped me to begin understanding how spectacular my Savior truly is and how pathetically weak my faith had become. I had sought but a very small remnant of His enormous power and consequently received only small blessing. Weak faith produces weak blessing; weak blessing, in turn, produces more weak faith. It's a vicious cycle that, if not halted, will drive you straight into the ground.

If you find yourself in a difficult spot today, don't do as I did and blame God. The difficulty was my own creation. I'm the one who ran, not Him. I'm the one who initiated the cycle and then perpetuated it.

Thankfully, there was a way to halt it. Chuck showed me that I needed to surrender and place Jesus on the throne!

From the outside looking in, pulling out the white flag and waving it is a scary proposition. At least it was for me. You are being asked to believe in the intangible, to seek the unseen, to trust the inexplicable. And the tool with which one does all of this is nothing more than basic faith. It is a faith that banks on God being who He says He is: One who keeps His promises. It's a risk. But isn't that what faith is—reaching out not despite the uncertainty but because of it?

Chuck encouraged me to get into the game. After all, you have to play to score. Rather than let me live off the anecdotes of others, he pushed me to experience Christ's glory first hand. While it wasn't an easy decision, for it would require relinquishing control, I did just that and placed my complete trust in Jesus. I found 2 Corinthians 4:7-9 of great encouragement:

> But we have this treasure in earthen vessels, that the surpassing greatness of the power may be of God and not from ourselves; we are afflicted in every way, but not crushed; perplexed, but not despairing; persecuted, but not forsaken; struck down, but not destroyed.

From the inside looking out, it has been hands down the best risk I've ever taken. I just wonder why it took me so long to see the light. Walking with God is a wonderful thing. He does keep His promises! While not always easy, the journey has been and continues to be worthwhile. My life now has purpose and meaning, whereas before it was mere existence.

I can't think of a more appropriate way to close than with *The Solid Rock*. It's a powerful summary of a powerful Savior.

My hope is built on nothing less
Than Jesus' blood and righteousness;
I dare not trust the sweetest frame,
But wholly lean on Jesus' name.

Refrain:
On Christ, the solid Rock, I stand;
All other ground is sinking sand,
All other ground is sinking sand.

When darkness veils His lovely face,
I rest on His unchanging grace;
In every high and stormy gale,
My anchor holds within the veil.

His oath, His covenant, His blood,
Support me in the whelming flood;
When all around my soul gives way,
He then is all my hope and stay.

When He shall come with trumpet sound,
O, may I then in Him be found;
Dressed in His righteousness alone,
Faultless to stand before the throne.[12]

You have at your disposal every resource you need to lead a joyful life, irrespective of circumstance. I plead with you to seek refuge in the Lord. Jesus can indeed be your "hope" and "stay," even when all else "gives way." Allow Him to do a wonderful, miraculous work in your life. You won't regret it.

Contacting Us

If you would like more information on how to know this wonderful Savior, please write us at:

Normandale Baptist Church
c/o Rebuilder Ministries
4701 West 84th Street
Bloomington, MN 55437

Notes

1. Thomas Merton, *Run to the Mountain*. Quoted in Philip Yancey, *Rumors of Another World: What on Earth Are We Missing?* (Grand Rapids, MI: Zondervan, 2003), p. 111.
2. John Piper, *Desiring God: Meditations of a Christian Hedonist*. (Portland, OR: Multnomah, 1986), p. 43.
3. Mindy Berge, "Bitter Waters Made Sweet," 2000. Used by permission.
4. Philip Yancey, *Reaching for the Invisible God: What Can We Expect to Find?* (Grand Rapids, MI: Zondervan, 2000), p. 91.
5. Joseph Scriven, "What a Friend We Have in Jesus," 1855.
6. John Piper, "Treasuring Christ Together, Part One," (Sermon, Bethlehem Baptist Church, Minneapolis, MN, 7 Sept. 2003).
7. Philip Yancey, *Reaching for the Invisible God*, p. 20.
8. Bill Gothard, *Our Most Important Messages Grow Out of Our Greatest Weaknesses*. (Oak Brook, IL: Institute in Basic Youth Conflicts, 1978), p. 3.
9. Major Ian Thomas, (Seminar, Normandale Baptist Church, Bloomington, MN, 1994). Used by permission.

10. John Piper, *Desiring God*, pp. 13-14.
11. Ron Hamilton, "Rejoice in the Lord," (Majesty Music Inc., 1978). Used by permission.
12. Edward Mote, "The Solid Rock," 1834.

Printed in the United States
30941LVS00001B/149